VICTORIA

VICTORIA
Crown Jewel of British Columbia

Susan Mayse

Photography by Chris Cheadle

Harbour Publishing

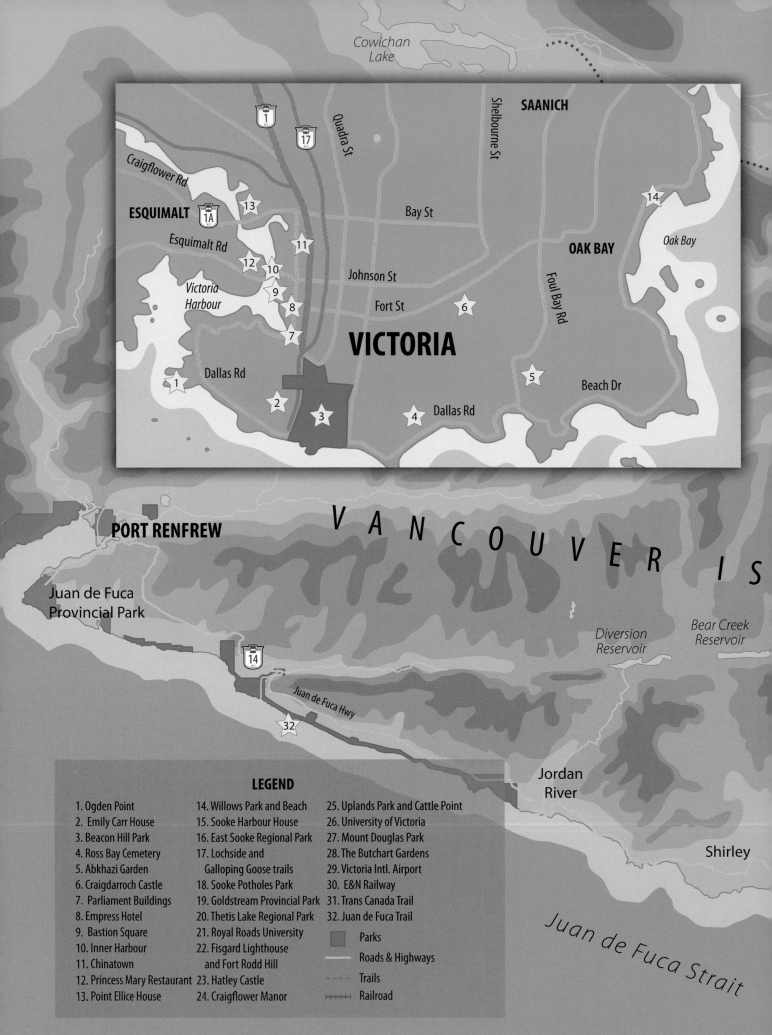

LEGEND

1. Ogden Point
2. Emily Carr House
3. Beacon Hill Park
4. Ross Bay Cemetery
5. Abkhazi Garden
6. Craigdarroch Castle
7. Parliament Buildings
8. Empress Hotel
9. Bastion Square
10. Inner Harbour
11. Chinatown
12. Princess Mary Restaurant
13. Point Ellice House

14. Willows Park and Beach
15. Sooke Harbour House
16. East Sooke Regional Park
17. Lochside and
    Galloping Goose trails
18. Sooke Potholes Park
19. Goldstream Provincial Park
20. Thetis Lake Regional Park
21. Royal Roads University
22. Fisgard Lighthouse
    and Fort Rodd Hill
23. Hatley Castle
24. Craigflower Manor

25. Uplands Park and Cattle Point
26. University of Victoria
27. Mount Douglas Park
28. The Butchart Gardens
29. Victoria Intl. Airport
30. E&N Railway
31. Trans Canada Trail
32. Juan de Fuca Trail

Parks

Roads & Highways

Trails

Railroad

Page 1: Cherry blossoms frame a totem pole outside Mungo Martin House in Thunderbird Park in the Royal BC Museum Cultural Precinct.

Pages 2–3: At twilight a rare tranquility touches the Inner Harbour and the Parliament Buildings beyond.

This spread: Fisgard Lighthouse, built in 1860, is seven years older than Canada.

Contents

Victoria and Its Region: Home Port

1

On a sunny day in February

waves scatter light across the Inner Harbour and sailboat rigging clatters in an onshore breeze. A low tide raises pungent scents of seaweed and long-vanished mud flats. Down on the stone causeway and the small-boat dock, people shelter below the wind to watch a musician lean over her guitar like a stray migratory bird. A few out-of-season tourists pause on the steps, but her main audience is office workers delving into their bag lunches.

Victoria's iconic tulips and daffodils are in flower everywhere, the cherry and plum trees are

a froth of pink blossoms, and while the rest of Canada shovels snow, here on southern Vancouver Island it's early spring.

Arriving at this harbour during the winter, visitors find, is like sailing back into summer. People snuggle up in fleece and rain gear, but only locals would admit to being chilly. They all look quite comfortable with their Murchie's coffee mugs and Munro's book bags. Sitting on the granite steps of the Inner Harbour, everyone is an islander and everyone is home.

A ferry tied up across the harbour sounds its whistle for departure, a seaplane taxis in on its watery runway and the musician glances at the time. As she packs up, a few loonies and toonies jingle into her guitar case, and then she skips up the stone stairs toward Wharf Street. The office workers trudge back to the Parliament Buildings—as old-school Victorians, mindful of their Crown colony past, call the Legislative Buildings—and the tourists drift away to the shops or the great stone Fairmont Empress Hotel presiding over the causeway.

The Inner Harbour is the gate to the city's heart. All day it buzzes with boat motors and whistles as water taxis scoot from jetty to jetty, seaplanes land and take off, and ferries dock and cast off. Yet sometimes it falls quiet. Then, the scent of tar and the gentle slap of waves pour Victoria's past back into the harbour like a rising tide: a prosperous First Nations village; a fur-trade fort with orders to protect an empire's sovereignty; a quieter harbour shared by working tugs, sailing ships and Canadian Pacific steamships; an older city of raw lumber and brick; a deepwater seaport perfectly located to trade in tea, spices, silks, furs, lumber and coal.

Two centuries ago, aboriginal residents of the south island and the first European explorers saw golden meadows of Garry oak and blue camas flowers sloping gently uphill from a creek estuary that wandered though tidal flats. Today, above the stone causeway, visitors see busy Government Street alive with pedestrians, cyclists, pedal cabs, Tally-Ho wagons and horse-drawn carriages, cars and buses, all the way from the windy southern sea cliffs to the northern outskirts of downtown Victoria.

Following pages: The Fairmont Empress Hotel presides over the Inner Harbour.

Seaplanes fly from Victoria's Inner Harbour to Vancouver and other nearby destinations. Floathomes line the dock fingers at Fisherman's Wharf across the harbour.

Above: Ornamental trees blossom in Beacon Hill Park while snow still covers much of Canada.

Opposite: Victorian-era mansions once lined the streets of James Bay, Victoria's oldest residential neighbourhood. Grand old houses still stand, especially in James Bay, Fernwood, Rockland and Oak Bay.

Visitors come to experience the Victoria that local residents all too often take for granted: ornamental and fruit trees that begin flowering as early as January, the sea view along many kilometres of waterfront walking paths, self-guided or commercial garden tours, seafood—including English-style fish and chips—that rivals the best anywhere, leisurely afternoon teas, professional and high-end amateur theatre, a vast selection of visual arts in public and private galleries, and live music in an astonishing range of genres from medieval and classical to ska.

A surprising number of Victoria's most interesting goings-on can be admired or sampled for free. An afternoon of window-shopping for antiques, touring commercial art galleries or visiting all the crafts stalls at the Bastion Square public market will cost you nothing but time. Live music performances at sea level on the Inner Harbour's lower causeway accept silver donations or just applause. Of course, a splendid high tea for two at the famous Empress Hotel will set you back about $100, but every customer who wanders into Silk Road nine blocks north is greeted at the door with a freshly brewed bowl of tea.

Small is Beautiful

Victoria is a small gem of historic brick and stone buildings and tasteful modern architecture among leafy squares and bright flower beds. It's a non-stop photo op and an open invitation to walk a few streets over to breakfast or cycle 10 klicks for an afternoon outing. The most venerable buildings occupy only a few square blocks—tourism promoters increasingly call this the "old town"—from the Inner Harbour to Chinatown. It is surrounded by a downtown core that eases into residential neighbourhoods, commercial districts or seashore a kilometre or so in any direction.

A totem pole overlooks the Parliament Buildings' lawns, where civil servants sometimes eat their lunch on the grass elbow to elbow with protesters challenging government policy.

Nestled up against Victoria's boundaries lie its three oldest sister municipalities, which for more than a century have stoutly resisted amalgamation.

Esquimalt carries the tang of salt air, and its century-and-a-half romance with the sea and its trades—particularly the Pacific Fleet of the Royal Canadian Navy—has cast up a jetsam of nautical and marine themes onto its streets and parks.

Oak Bay, on the east side of Victoria, preserves the flower-strewn oak meadows that provided its name in Uplands Park, a naturalist's delight, while its English-looking "high street" and narrow wynds enclose some of the region's most charming residential areas. People in Oak Bay really do amble out for afternoon tea and crumpets, fish and chips, fine British ales on tap, fresh sushi or handmade Italian deli sandwiches, and it's hard to avoid the word "quaint" in describing its sunny southerly neighbourhoods.

Saanich, the largest and most varied of the core municipalities, retains scattered patches of the farmland that settlers from the 1840s onward cleared for orchards, bees, grain, livestock and vegetable crops. Its largely residential neighbourhoods were once popular destinations for holiday tram outings to Cadboro Bay or Cordova Bay, but these days they house students and staff of the University of Victoria (half of which lies in Oak Bay) in settings that range from village centre to deeply rural.

Outward again from the core lie the other municipalities and electoral areas that help make up Greater Victoria and the Capital Regional District (CRD).

First Peoples

Archeologists believe the ancestors of the modern aboriginal people on southern Vancouver Island arrived at least 5,000 years ago, overland and possibly also by sea from northern Asia, though this date keeps getting pushed earlier as new sites and artifacts come to light.

Ever since the last ice age, this area has been a natural paradise, one that abundantly provided Native peoples with all that was necessary for a relatively easy and comfortable life, with enough

Finlayson Arm and Saanich Inlet separate the Saanich Peninsula from the rest of the south island.

surplus wealth to create a rich, complex culture. This is a region that, for time out of mind, First Peoples have lived in. They have harvested its abundant foods and gathered its raw materials to create homes and clothing and tools. Even the smallest tools and weapons found at the earliest sites are beautifully ergonomic in design and often bear ornamentation. The people who shaped these objects had time to make them not only highly functional but beautiful. Native people have named geographical features, preserved information about significant places and retold stories about the area that explain their mythic origins. Many would agree that the greatest wealth that this bountiful land made possible is the long tradition of visual arts, dance, song and storytelling.

Today the Pacheedaht, T'Sou-ke (Sooke), Scia'new, Lekwungen (Esquimalt and Songhees), Malahat and Wsanec (Saanich) people occupy lands throughout the region, but the aboriginal presence permeates far deeper and stretches wider than the visible communities. You can visit the bighouse in the Royal BC Museum Cultural Precinct, browse Native art and craft shops or admire the towering totem pole on Songhees Point from anywhere around the Inner Harbour, but those are only the most obvious reminders.

Every place has its name, and every name has its story. That past will always be here, as First Peoples will always be here; others may come and go, but this is their home. This is first and always their place, and every influence on the land over the past two centuries—however sweeping it seems—is a thin veneer of recent change. Beyond and beneath what meets the casual gaze, a world of long-standing tradition and lore quietly continues.

Good landing beaches used by these seagoing peoples have multi-layered shell middens, like those at Turkey Head or Esquimalt Lagoon. Artifacts from excavations are on display in the Royal BC Museum and elsewhere, and sometimes archeological digs call for volunteers.

Oak meadows in the region have burial cairns or firepits where people roasted their camas bulbs. In fact aboriginal people maintained these grassy meadows over many generations with controlled burns to remove shrubs so the blue-flowered camas could grow freely. You may come across a camas roast at Beacon Hill or another spot some summer afternoon, absorb local lore, get

Start paddling as young as these boys, and the fine art of balancing a dugout canoe comes naturally.

woodsmoke in your hair and taste the sweet, starchy bulbs. In stands of old-growth cedar you can spot where trees have been harvested for bark or felled for canoe or house building. Several parks and wildlife preserves offer workshops, talks and guided or self-guided walking tours.

An Evolving Landscape

Seen from space, the Victoria region is clearly identifiable as the southeastern tip of Vancouver Island. The area stretches from the logging and fishing village of Port Renfrew out on the wind-swept west coast of Vancouver Island, all the way east across the forested Malahat Ridge to the head of Saanich Inlet, north to include the Saanich Peninsula and south to densely populated Victoria, Esquimalt and Oak Bay. However, Greater Victoria is an idea rather than a political entity, so its size and boundaries vary depending on the source; Statistics Canada lists the land area as 2,342 square kilometres (about 904 square miles), slightly smaller than the nations of Luxembourg or Samoa.

Great glaciers ground and polished the land in several long cycles, as two floes moved south over southern Vancouver Island and slightly to the west or east; the weight of the ice pushed the land mass down by 150 to 300 metres (roughly 500 to 1,000 feet). When the climate started to warm about 14,000 years ago, the ice sheets melted and the land rebounded from the weight of ice, exposing land that had been submerged until the sea settled at its present level. Glacial till left behind when the ice melted would eventually support vegetation, and meltwater formed the first lakes and streams.

The landscape we know, which developed only in the last six thousand years, has produced mature forests dominated by fir, cedar, hemlock and maple. Victoria's gently rolling Garry oak meadows are punctuated by rocky heights, and on the Saanich Peninsula interior ridges and hills

Opposite: Heavy rainfall recharges the creeks of the Juan de Fuca Trail rainforest.

The Mystic Beach waterfall sends an arc of fresh water directly into the sea. Beaches and parks on the West Shore offer spectacular settings for hikes, picnics and camping.

A rower ventures into the autumn mist at Elk Lake, where Canada's Olympic rowing team trains.

Opposite: A classic sailboat takes advantage of a light breeze off Sidney.

overlook a coastal plain. West Shore and West Coast areas tend to be rocky and steep, with dark volcanic outcrops to show their ancient origins; between the cliffs and outcrops lie many lush grassy or wooded valleys and a scattering of pretty lakes. This diverse geography produces equally diverse microclimates, from sunny summers in the southern areas of Oak Bay, Victoria, the Peninsula and Metchosin to cooler days and heavy rainfall in Port Renfrew, Goldstream and Highlands.

Water shaped this terrain over many geological phases, and today salt water and fresh water define most elements of it. The open Pacific scours its exposed western and southern shores, and Haro Strait washes its more sheltered eastern beaches. Lakes and marshes dot the landscape in low-lying areas, sustaining wildlife and offering spectacular walks, swimming, picnic areas and viewpoints. Dozens of rivers and streams cast a shining net across the gently folding landscape, many visible but some now lost (but not forgotten) under commercial or residential development. Environmental groups have worked hard in recent years to "daylight," or restore, these lost streams.

In 1907 English writer Rudyard Kipling visited Victoria during a lecture tour of Canada and wrote home to his family, "Real estate agents recommend it as a little piece of England—the island on which it stands is about the size of Great Britain—but no England is set in any such seas or so fully charged with the mystery of the larger ocean beyond."

A delightful countryside folds and curves between these waters in a vast patchwork of green forest interspersed with tawny bedrock and rich brown ploughland. Three major formations—the Sooke Hills, the Highlands and the Malahat Ridge—separate Greater Victoria from "up-island," which stretches northwest for another 400 kilometres (250 miles). Forested ridges and hills also rise from the Saanich Peninsula as it extends northward from the urban core, sheltering long,

sinuous Saanich Inlet, where every day recreational boaters and working vessels scrawl their white wakes across the blue waters. Visible just offshore to the east lie the scattered jewels of the Gulf Islands, a recreational and residential paradise halfway between Vancouver Island and the mainland city of Vancouver.

These boundaries seem reassuring and natural to islanders, who tend to orient themselves with coastline, parks, rivers or hills. If you ask for directions in Victoria and are sensibly told to drive three kilometres east to Cadboro Bay, for example, you may be talking to a transplanted Calgarian with a well-tuned internal compass; a local will probably tell you to drive past Mount Tolmie, turn left after the golf course and go on downhill till you see a beach.

In this part of Vancouver Island, we can cross-country ski, climb rock faces or small mountains, hike, cycle, trail-ride, canoe the rivers and lakes, kayak or sail the ocean, explore an endlessly diverse natural history and photograph views now famous for their changeable beauty. A network of long-distance cycling and walking trails—the Galloping Goose, Lochside, Trans Canada and E&N Rail trails—passes through most of the region's municipalities. All of this lies within a one- or two-hour drive of Victoria's Inner Harbour.

The Lochside Trail on the Saanich Peninsula links to a network of cycling and walking trails across the south island.

Sports and outdoor activities are popular on the south island. Golfers from colder climates appreciate the long snow-free days on several world-class courses. Field sports, racquet sports and many others support local amateur and professional teams and regularly welcome touring teams and exhibition games. Leisurely cricket, a legacy of the British Empire, and hair-trigger-fast lacrosse, derived from an aboriginal ball-and-racquet game, have two things in common: they're better represented in the Victoria region than in many places, and they both make a fascinating way to while away an afternoon as a spectator. Those with a taste for intensity can take part in polo, catch-and-release fly-fishing, windsurfing, zip-lining—sliding down an aerial wire in a body harness attached to a pulley—and bungy jumping. Well-known athletes from the area include basketball star Steve Nash, international rugby sensation Gareth Rees and Olympic rower Silken Laumann.

The region's historical and cultural landscape is as rich and varied as its physical geography. The McPherson Playhouse and the ornate Royal Theatre in downtown Victoria are the traditional venues for touring professional theatre companies and musicians, and Langham Court Theatre, tucked away in Rockland, has been a lively and respected community theatre since the 1930s. The Belfry Theatre started producing contemporary work in 1976 in inner-city Fernwood.

Painters, sculptors and other visual artists have always appreciated the south island's mild climate and easygoing lifestyle, and among the well-known artists in the region are Richard Hunt, Charles Elliott, Pat Martin Bates, Ted Harrison and Phyllis Serota. Musicians range from the home-grown talent of superstars Nelly Furtado and David Foster to indie rockers Jets Overhead, Hot Hot Heat and Immaculate Machine. Radio star Vicki Gabereau attended Oak Bay High School. Well-known writers include poets Patrick Lane, Lorna Crozier and Susan Musgrave and novelists Jack Hodgins and Marilyn Bowering.

The University of Victoria, evolving from Victoria College, officially moved in 1967 from its original 1915 building to airy new buildings on the site of the one-time Gordon Head army camp. UVic regularly places among Canada's top-ranking universities for sciences, humanities and other disciplines, and is often cited as Canada's loveliest campus for its architecture, welcoming open spaces and flourishing gardens. Another south island university, Royal Roads, occupies the high Edwardian building and manicured grounds of Hatley Castle. Other institutions include Camosun College, which occupies UVic's grand old building at the former Victoria College campus, and several business, art and design colleges.

Far left: The 17th hole at Olympic View Golf Club in Metchosin.

Left: UVic is known for academic excellence—and bunny rabbits.

Below: Fall leaves frame Hatley Castle in Colwood, the home of Royal Roads University.

Top: Cattle Point offers a prospect of the Oak Bay waterfront.

Above: A mule deer buck surveys his domain in Gowlland Tod Park in the Highlands.

Forecast: More Sunshine and Natural Beauty

Southern Vancouver Island's worst-kept secret is its mild climate, with its long slow springs, mild winters and playful sea breezes. Often compared to the Mediterranean, the area gets a generous dollop of sunshine, about 2,200 hours every year; in comparison, Vancouver gets about 1,900 hours. Moisture-laden air from the Pacific flows right over the island's mountain spine to fall on the mainland instead, so the Victoria area gets only about 600 mm (24 inches) of rainfall annually, compared to Vancouver's 1,219 mm (48 inches) and Seattle's 970 mm (38 inches).

Drought might seem strange in a place bounded and dimpled and crisscrossed by water, known for its mists and fogs and gentle rains, but since most of the rain falls in the winter, the region can also have extremely dry summers. Water shortages and rationing occur regularly, forcing homeowners and businesses to limit their usage. Some lush rural gardens sprout signs that announce "irrigated by well water" to deflect claims that they're cheating.

More than two hundred frost-free days, about seven months' worth, are a gift to local gardeners. The renowned Butchart Gardens occupy a former stone quarry on the Saanich Peninsula, and Abkhazi Garden fills a Victoria backyard. Smaller public and private gardens of all kinds brighten the streets. Palm trees and yuccas flourish alongside native and introduced temperate-zone trees and flowers and the region's best-known native trees, the arbutus and the Garry oak.

A twisted arbutus tree with smooth russet bark peeling away to reveal new golden-green bark, crowned in glossy green deciduous leaves, perched on a rocky outcrop above a dark blue sea—for many, that says everything about southern Vancouver Island. Some people think arbutus trees are dying when the red bark peels and sloughs off in long strips on a summer breeze, but it's all part of the tree's natural cycle. Arbutuses thrive in thin dry soil and will grow on bluffs that offer little foothold or nourishment. Grassy meadows are ringed with the Garry oak trees that gave Oak Bay its name more than a century ago.

Autumn brings its own beauty to the Japanese Garden, one of the earliest areas developed at the Butchart Gardens.

Garry oak and arbutus, among other native species, are now recognized as vital to our local ecology and are protected from needless removal. However, not everyone loves these stately sentinels, which shed leaves and occasionally branches. Some homeowners prefer well tamed lawns and borders of introduced shrubs and flowers, and people who originally come from more open landscapes can feel oppressively hemmed in by our forest trees. However, naturalists gravitate to this region, and homegrown naturalists grow up aware of the wealth of animal life around them. Bears amble through rural parks. Cougars turn up in city parkades and backyards. Raccoons and deer are tame enough to risk wearing out their welcome. Ponds and marshes teem with frogs, newts and salamanders, and every pocket park and backyard flutters with migrant and resident birds.

Certain familiar Canadian species have never found their way to Vancouver Island. Not everyone regrets the absence of skunk and resident grizzly bears (a few grizzlies have visited the northern part of the island), but some miss the magpie, chipmunk, coyote, porcupine, lynx and fox. Constant marine traffic in the Inner Harbour and its waterways doesn't keep away seals, river otters, porpoises, fish and other marine animals. A few residents require a watchful eye, including the black widow spider. Pests such as clothes moths, fleas and wood-devouring ants all flourish in the warm climate. At the cost of minor irritation, though, these species provide great opportunities for observation and study.

Left: The Pacific dogwood is British Columbia's flower emblem.

Above: Shedding its red bark is part of an arbutus tree's life cycle.

The south island's natural beauty inevitably has nourished a strong, activist environmental movement. There's the large, venerable Victoria Natural History Society, founded in 1944, as well as scores of smaller and more recent groups, which often specialize in one habitat or concern. Notable locals include environmentalist Vicky Husband and UVic climate change expert Dr. Andrew Weaver.

Yet the real Victoria, true to its Taoist influences, is not just the Victoria you see. The real Victoria region sizzles and shouts with daring new technology, a small but imaginative industrial base, cutting-edge fine arts, world-changing music, a vibrant ethnic mosaic and a cosmopolitan cultural life. It just happens to be surpassingly beautiful as well.

And despite all of this innovation, an old-world, shabby-genteel elegance overlays the natural splendour of this new-world island in the western sea. Even the region's gritty industrial areas and humbler residential neighbourhoods somehow conjure up a scatty, tatty charm. On mild, rainy winter evenings, the golden light from cozy cafés and one-of-a-kind shops reflects out onto the wet sidewalks; in the long violet-tinged twilight of mild summer evenings, laughter and music drifts from the terraces and parks where people gather to savour the last light.

Opposite: Grey whales migrate north and south along the coasts of Vancouver Island.

Victoria: A Perfect Eden

dancing with blue camas flowers, alive with bird-song, trickling with streams and springs, deeply cut by natural harbours and quiet waterways, rich in fish and wildlife: to the First Nations this has been home for millennia. The Songhees people who lived around the Inner Harbour area of central Victoria called it Camosun, Camosack or Camossung, meaning

"rush of water" in their Lekwungen dialect of the Northern Straits Salish language. The name refers to a place on the Gorge Waterway, the navigable channel that winds between low banks to flow into the harbour. Fresh water and salt water used to mingle there, in a short waterfall that reversed direction with each change of tide, until rocks were removed from the narrows.

Songhees lands manager Cheryl Bryce wrote, "After the flood, the transformer, Haylas, was travelling with Raven and Mink teaching the people how things were to be done." They met a young girl named Camossung who was hungry and offered her a choice of foods. "She refused many things but duck, herring, coho, and oyster she accepted, and that is why these were plentiful on the Gorge waterway. Because she was greedy, Haylas told her she would look after the food resources for her people and he turned her and her grandfather into stone."

Today's city of Victoria overlooks much of the beautiful and bountiful area that has supported aboriginal people for so many years. Natural history and human history layer thickly in long-inhabited areas; much of central Victoria's landscape is heavily altered. The creek that flowed into the harbour and its tidal flats lie beneath the grounds of the Empress Hotel, and the wooden bridge that crossed the bay has given way to a substantial stone causeway and quays. The Songhees, Haida and Clallam villages that sprang up around the harbour at various times have vanished, now replaced by ornate Edwardian buildings and modern glass towers. Present-day resources lean to information technology, commerce and culture rather than fish, shellfish and waterfowl, but the Gorge Waterway is still the city's main artery and a cherished locale for its parks, scenic walkways, boating and waterfront homes.

Three Songhees village sites once bordered the Inner Harbour: one at James Bay near the present Empress Hotel, one at the site of today's Parliament Buildings and one at Pallastsis (or Songhees) Point, across the harbour from the legislature. Pallastsis, meaning "the place of the cradle," is where parents would place their children's cradles after they learned to walk, to ensure a long life. The harbour mud flats supported fine clam beds until they were dredged and filled for the construction of lower Government Street and the Empress Hotel. Nearby at Beacon Hill, the Songhees people regularly burned off trees and shrubs to create grassy meadows for the profusion of camas plants; the camas bulbs that they roasted every summer were an important food source. Farther away from the harbour, cedar trees provided wood for dugout canoes of all sizes and bark and roots to weave ropes, fishing lines, baskets, clothing and other household items. The Songhees lived well in a carefully managed, sustainable landscape.

First Nations in the region signed treaties with Hudson's Bay Company Chief Factor James Douglas (later Sir James Douglas, governor of the colony of Vancouver Island and eventually British Columbia) in the mid-19th century, some of which are currently under review. The Lekwungen people also had villages at Sitchamalth ("drift logs in sand") or Willows Beach, at Sungayka ("snow patches") or Cadboro Bay, and at other sites around the south island. Seventy years after the Hudson's Bay Company set up shop on the Inner Harbour, the Songhees and Esquimalt people were confined to two reserves in View Royal. Like aboriginal people elsewhere, they suffered from the loss of their lands and livelihoods, complicated by the ravages of several smallpox epidemics and the banning of the potlatch and other traditional ceremonies.

Camosun College students and instructors participate in the annual Camas Roast at the Lansdowne Campus, 2009. Images courtesy Camosun College

Traditional dugout canoes line the beach at Old Songhees Village during a potlatch, 1872. Richard Maynard photograph. Image AA-00100 courtesy of Royal BC Museum, BC Archives

A walkway now skirts the site of the old Songhees village on Victoria Harbour.

Recent generations, however, have achieved a striking revival of their arts, culture, social networks and education. Today's Lekwungen people work with their elders and teach young people traditional skills: gathering and cooking foods; making canoes, paddles and other tools; and practising traditional art forms including music, dance, woodcarving and painting. They also play an active part in the life of the city around them and advise institutions including the University of Victoria and Camosun College on how best to provide educational opportunities for their young people.

Explorers and Settlers

Artists portrayed Vancouver Island landscapes, including Fort Victoria, as a reflection of familiar European scenes. Image PDP-02174 courtesy of Royal BC Museum, BC Archives

Chinese explorers may have visited the west coast of North America in the 5th century AD, and Japanese sailors travelled here in the late 16th century, around the same time as the first Europeans. Francis Drake may have sailed this far north in 1579, though the records are far from clear, and Spanish explorers—Manuel Quimper in 1790 and Francisco de Eliza and José María Narváez in 1791—may have been the first Europeans to visit the southern tip of Vancouver Island.

Early European visitors coming from a domesticated landscape of grimy cities and bleak factories first experienced the south island's mild Mediterranean climate, rich forest-bred soils and long growing season as a paradise. The Hudson's Bay Company built a fort here in 1843 to exploit the wealth of furs and to strengthen the British presence on the west coast of North America, to prevent expansion by the United States. Chief Factor James Douglas called the southern tip of the island "a perfect Eden in the midst of the dreary wilderness."

Fort Camosun, as the HBC first called their fur-trade fort, hugged the gentle slope rising from

the Inner Harbour at the foot of today's Fort Street. The timber palisade and buildings, built by Songhees people in exchange for trade goods, were dismantled a generation later. They gave way first to wooden buildings—lost in a succession of devastating fires—and later to brick and stone buildings, some of which still stand on Wharf Street and in Bastion Square. The square marks the location of the fort's three-storey octagonal north bastion. In 1843 the HBC expediently honoured the young queen of England by changing the name of Fort Camosun to Fort Victoria.

By the 1850s, despite Douglas's attempts to attract settlers, only a few hundred newcomers lived in and around Fort Victoria. Most were HBC workers of English, Scots, Québécois, Métis, First Nations and Hawaiian descent. James Douglas himself was "a Scotch West Indian," the son of a freed black woman in British Guiana and a Glasgow merchant. As a boy he was sent to Scotland for his education before joining the North West Company at 16 and later the HBC; his wife Amelia was of partially aboriginal ancestry. As chief factor and later as governor of the Colony of Vancouver Island, Douglas championed justice and ethnic rights: he invited freed slaves from the United States to homestead and promptly settled treaties with all 10 First Nations in the Victoria region, between 1850 and 1852.

Early Victoria had an ethnically mixed, multilingual population that generally got along in uneasy tolerance, with only occasional friction. The injustices would horrify today's residents, but for its time it was a relatively progressive and tolerant society. Efforts to build up the immigrant population continued to progress slowly, however, and Britain's claim still barely had a toehold on Vancouver Island.

In 1858 the discovery of gold in the Fraser River Valley changed everything. Victoria was the port of entry for the British Columbia goldfields. Its muddy streets and ravines sprouted a temporary "Canvas-town" of more than 20,000 would-be millionaires from every part of the world, many of them veterans of gold rushes in California and Australia, en route to the Fraser River and soon afterward to a new gold strike in the Cariboo town of Barkerville. The throng included Chinese miners and railway labourers who had stayed on in Victoria, creating a neighbourhood they called Huabu ("Chinese Port") in the area of present-day Chinatown. But the population explosion increased racist discrimination and violence, and under threat, many black settlers left. In the 1860s the Confederate flag flew everywhere, and the US Civil War was fought and refought on the sawdust floors of Johnson Street taverns; for a while it must have seemed that every spare Southern spy was undercover in Victoria. No longer could the Songhees people and a handful of newcomers bask unheeded in their sunny meadows and paddle in the cool Gorge water. The rest of the world had discovered Victoria.

Top: Canada's oldest Chinese cemetery, a national historic site, occupies Harling Point.

Above: St. Ann's Academy offered an education to aboriginal and nonaboriginal girls for more than a century. Now the fine old buildings and grounds are popular for concerts and weddings.

Downtown

The city has flourished ever since, right through another great gold rush in the Yukon, epidemics, booms, busts, two world wars and wave after wave of immigration. Victoria is now a resplendent small city of hidden—but discoverable—treasures. History underlies every step of Victoria's streets and its venerable buildings, and those who learn to look past the additions, alterations and renovations can still soak it in.

The first expansion outside the fort's palisade was in the downtown area, which the Songhees called Kuo-sing-el-as, or "place of strong fibre," for the willow trees growing there—their inner bark was used to make fishing lines. Songhees bighouses once lined the shoreline from Pallastsis (Songhees Point) up to the present-day Blue Bridge, properly called the Johnson Street Bridge.

While the Songhees moved their village from the Inner Harbour west to Esquimalt in 1911, you can appreciate their thriving culture by visiting the Royal BC Museum. Also located at sites around traditional Songhees territory are seven large sculptures by artist Butch Dick that represent a woman's spindle whorl for spinning wool. An informational display at each site describes Songhees life and culture.

Victoria's population—about 83,000 in 2009—occupies a compact 19.68 square kilometres (7.6 square miles) area fanning out from the Inner Harbour. In an average year, more than three million people visit the region and spend just over a billion dollars. Tourism drives Victoria's economy.

Downtown Victoria—overlooking the harbour and loosely bounded by Wharf, Blanshard, Humboldt and Fisgard streets—is a compact area that even the most leisurely walker can cross in minutes. On sunny summer afternoons it teems with cruise ship passengers and day visitors trekking from shop to restaurant to tourist attraction. At street level, buskers vie with food vendors and sidewalk artists for the attention of passersby.

A glance upward to the second and third storeys is rewarding, since elaborate cornices, window settings and friezes decorate many of the heritage buildings. Three pretty squares—Bastion, Centennial and Market—host flourishing businesses, pocket parks occupy odd corners, and flower baskets and planters are everywhere. Victoria's oldest churches, businesses, homes and cemeteries are clustered in the Inner Harbour area, and the district is said to be richly haunted.

One treasure hidden in plain view in downtown Victoria is the Union Club of BC. Founded in 1879 on the model of English gentlemen's clubs, it has weathered many humorous broadsides at its stuffy and outdated traditions. These days the joke is on the scoffers, since the club has adapted and progressed to become the sole survivor of a handful of such clubs that sprang up in the late 19th century. The Union Club welcomed founding members that included Jews and Catholics,

Waiting for a customer, a pedicab driver gets a chance to relax near the Empress Hotel.

Bastion Square in a rare quiet mood; arts and crafts stalls jam the main square on summer days.

unlike other clubs of its day, and it later accepted women and men of any background who paid their dues and behaved with decorum. This and its relatively respectful treatment of staff may have sailed it between the shoals of changing times and economic downturns. Today the Union Club provides dining and accommodation for out-of-town members, reciprocal members of other clubs and other visitors. Rarely it hosts a public function; if you attend one, take the chance to admire the harbour view and the architectural graces of the "new" 1913 building on Gordon Street.

Exploring Victoria's Oldest Neighbourhoods

Many people who visit Victoria for a day or two never get beyond the Inner Harbour, downtown or old town, and while these areas have their charms, they can be touristy. An hour's walk in any direction will take you through Victoria's oldest districts and neighbourhoods tourists rarely see. Or for the price of a couple of T-shirts you can take a horse-drawn carriage ride or bicycle-powered Kabuki cab ride along Victoria's waterfront, through parks and down quiet back streets.

In the old town, only a few blocks from the Inner Harbour, you can visit the Royal BC Museum on Belleville Street or the Maritime Museum of BC in Bastion Square. You can also sample fine baking and light lunches at old favourites including the Dutch Bakery on Fort Street or Murchie's Tea & Coffee on Government Street, sample handmade treats at Roger's Chocolates on Government Street or try a vegetarian meal at Rebar on Bastion Square. The old town and downtown are also where you can take part in seasonal celebrations: Chinese New Year in January or February, the Swiftsure International Yacht Race in May, JazzFest in June, Ska Fest in July, the Dragon Boat Festival and the floating musical event Symphony Splash in August, and the Classic Boat Festival

Following pages: The annual Symphony Splash gives the Inner Harbour a new view of water music.

Left: Rebar remains one of Victoria's favourite vegetarian restaurants.

Above: The Royal BC Museum and provincial archives overlook a reflecting pool.

Top: Gate of Harmonious Interest marks the entrance to Victoria's Chinatown.

Above: Fan Tan Alley is home to several happily offbeat shops.

and the Fringe Festival in September, among others. Live music is on tap year-round in bars, night-clubs and auditoriums.

Victoria's oldest business, industrial and residential districts are now ageing gracefully. Not far from the downtown core, most neighbourhoods provide a pleasant, safe stroll on tree-lined streets of well-kept homes and gardens. Even the smallest garret apartments often have blooming flowerpots on their stair landings, and many houses have flourishing vegetable or flower gardens spilling out toward the sidewalk. A few are in serious disrepair, as you'd expect in any area with a long history, but most look lovingly lived in.

Jumbled among the houses are specialty shops, historic sites, bookstores, art galleries, corner stores and parks that range from a grassy patch with a tiny flower bed to a full-blown sports and recreation centre with a baseball diamond, Olympic-sized pool, jogging track and soccer field. Why keep life's pleasures at a distance when they could be next door? Even with a shrinking pension or a student's shoestring budget, Victorians can enjoy a beach outing or a scenic hike for at most the cost of a bus ticket.

A 10-minute walk up Government Street will bring you to the modern-day Chinatown. You can't really miss your left-hand turn onto Fisgard Street, since it passes beneath the monumental red- and gold-tiled Gate of Harmonious Interest. Built in China in 1981 and given to the city of Victoria, the gate bears complex and beautiful carvings to reinforce its theme of joy, prosperity and unity. Two stone lions flank the gate to protect Chinatown, and bells hang at each corner to ward off evil spirits.

At the turn of the last century, Chinatown stretched from the old Johnson Street ravine, now filled to support Market Square, to Herald Street and beyond, overhung with then-legal opium smoke and, at least to non-residents, an air of mystery. Many interconnecting alleys and tiny courtyards allowed gamblers to flee police raids. One of the few survivors is narrow Fan Tan Alley, named for a popular Chinese dice game, which is still a handy shortcut and home to several happily offbeat shops. In the block above Government Street stands the Chinese Public School, a tall brick building with graceful curved eaves. Built by the Chinese community in 1909 when Chinese children were banned from Victoria's public schools unless they spoke English, the school still teaches Chinese language, history and culture. Victoria's Chinese population has long since scattered into outlying residential areas, but the crowded sidewalks, bright storefront displays, busy restaurants and bakeries still make Chinatown an intriguing place to visit.

It's especially exciting to visit for the annual Lion Dance during Chinese New Year festivities in January or February, when shops hang lettuce offerings outside their doors for the

The Chinese Public School still teaches Chinese culture after more than a century.

"lion" to nibble, and families give their children lucky money in brightly decorated red envelopes. A few people sniff at the stereotypes and the romanticizing of the bad old days, but the celebration is as much part of Victoria as the Robbie Burns banquets in January and the Greek Festival in September. The scents of Chinese firecrackers, incense and almond cookies linger from many Victorian childhoods.

Victoria's Congregation Emanu-El Synagogue on Blanshard Street is the oldest synagogue in Canada. Its cornerstone was laid in June 1863 during a celebration that must have been extraordinary for its time, even in hustling, polyglot gold-rush Victoria: the mayor and council, the chief justice, the Freemasons, the French Benevolent Society, the Hebrew Benevolent Society, the St. Andrew's Society and various choirs and bands all attended. Nuggets and grains from the northern goldfields helped pay for the building, since the first Jews arrived in 1858 en route to the Fraser River and Barkerville. A few stayed to found some of Victoria's most successful and long-lived businesses.

A half-hour walk west, then south and east, around Laurel Point will put you on a favourite waterfront walk past Fisherman's Wharf to Ogden Point, where the glittering, city-sized cruise ships tie up. A walk on the Ogden Point breakwater, made of huge concrete blocks, may take you past fishers trying for cod or stray salmon, scuba divers exploring the rich bottom life and photographers capturing the panoramic view of Victoria and Esquimalt harbours and the Olympic Range in Washington state, far across the Juan de Fuca Strait. Seaplanes landing at or taking off from the Inner Harbour pass low over the small lighthouse on the end of the breakwater, and pilot boats from the nearby pilot station race out to mid-strait to guide in cruise ships. The deepwater port also berths visiting naval vessels, freighters, cable-layers and other working ships. This is no place for

Floathomes of many shapes, sizes and colours line the dock at Fisherman's Wharf.

Previous pages: First Nations designs decorate the Ogden Point breakwater that attracts walkers and joggers; far beyond are the Olympic Mountains of Washington state.

anyone troubled by heights or unsteady of step, and despite perverse local custom it's not the best walk in heavy weather, with huge waves breaking overtop. Far better to storm-watch over coffee at Ogden Point Café, which has one of Victoria's better vegetarian menus.

This walk skirts the old residential neighbourhood of James Bay, which until a century ago was separated by streams and tidal mud flats from the business district; part of the area rests on landfill added for the construction of the Empress Hotel. A dogleg away from the water will take you

through sunny streets lined with a happy mixture of late Victorian houses, small and large, crumbling and lovingly restored, on modest lots. Many of these old houses dripping with gingerbread ornament on eaves and rooflines have survived well, but enterprising homeowners carry out ongoing renovations that make living here increasingly expensive. However, while James Bay is undergoing some gentrification, it remains largely a down-to-earth neighbourhood with a strong sense of community and history.

Another level two kilometres (1.2 miles) along Dallas Road through Holland Point Park will take you to the foot of Government Street. A few blocks inland at 207 Government is Emily Carr House, now a popular heritage site, where the famous Victoria artist and writer was born and grew up. Emily Carr was the first painter raised on the south island who knew no allegiance to old-

Freighters ply Juan de Fuca Strait bound for every part of the world.

world ways. Instead, she probed the heart of the land that shaped and nourished her.

Emily Carr was one of seven children of a Victoria merchant and spent most of her life in eastern James Bay. As a girl she played in wild Beacon Hill Park, and as a young woman she did the unthinkable, travelling alone up-coast to paint aboriginal settlements and stay in her new friends' bighouses; the Nuu-chah-nulth people named her Klee Wyck, "the laughing one." Her training at art schools in San Francisco, London and Paris taught her conventional techniques and painting styles, but Carr was driven to interpret her own island landscapes in her own way. Disdained by proper Victorians for her gypsy garb and her pet parrot, monkey and dogs, which she pushed

A sunny afternoon calls for a bike ride along Dallas Road.

Emily Carr and friends rest with caravan *Elephant* on sketching trip. Image B-09610 courtesy of Royal BC Museum, BC Archives

Emily Carr grew up in this charming house, now a historic site.

around James Bay in a baby carriage, she struggled to survive the Depression years as a boarding-house landlady and art teacher. Often she sold her paintings for a few dollars on the sidewalk. Late in her life, Canada's Group of Seven painters took an interest in Carr's work, and her distinctive style flowered into its full transformational vision.

A little farther north lies the yacht pond where generations of Victoria children have sailed their model boats around the resident mallard ducks or ice-skated during Victoria's rare freeze-ups. A few steps farther, beyond the wind-blasted evergreens, Mile 0 marks the western end of the Trans-Canada Highway. The unassuming stone-and-wood marker sits in a grassy triangle overlooking Juan de Fuca Strait near a statue of Marathon of Hope runner Terry Fox.

Following pages: A spinnaker start to the Swiftsure International Yacht Race.

Warmed by the Sun

Beacon Hill Park is the living green heart of Victoria, stretching from near the downtown core to the Dallas Road waterfront at Mile 0 and from Douglas Street to Cook Street. The hill that gives the park its name was once used to signal ships at sea, warning them of Brotchie Ledge, an offshore reef. For centuries the Songhees people had fortifications, houses, burial sites and cooking pits on the hill they called Meegan, or "warmed by the sun." Here they relaxed in the sun or played a hockey-style game called qoqwialls, and they regularly burned off trees and shrubs to create open ground for camas to grow. Every spring countless camas plants still carpet the slopes. Several early visitors compared the grassy height sloping down to the sea to a fragment of heaven, and James Douglas wrote that it almost seemed to have "dropped from the clouds." Douglas earmarked the area for parkland on an 1849 map, though cattle and pigs grazed there for a time, devastating the camas crop. It was set aside for a park in 1862, the same year the city of Victoria was incorporated, and turned over to the city in 1882.

Today beautifully manicured gardens and surviving or restored natural landscapes thrive amongst the park's approximately 74 hectares (184 acres) of native grassland, oak woods, outcroppings, shoreline vegetation, mixed forest and great swathes of seasonal wildflowers. Every book on walking in Victoria features Beacon Hill Park, and there are many signs throughout the park to guide visitors. The best plan is to go and explore it for yourself. You can easily spend a day roaming the park from boundary to boundary: observing birds and small animals, watching a few overs at the cricket pitch, visiting the children's petting zoo and stopping for a deliciously decadent burger or soft ice cream at the much-loved Beacon Drive-In restaurant nearby.

East of Beacon Hill Park, hip Cook Street Village rises southeastward to the shady streets of genteel Rockland, where many grand heritage homes overlook the more modest neighbourhood of Fairfield. The Rockland mansions include the BC Lieutenant-Governor's residence, Government House—where anyone can visit the well-tended gardens or join the volunteer gardeners—and Craigdarroch Castle, now a heritage site, which island coal baron Robert Dunsmuir promised to and built for his wife, Joan. Down closer to the sea in Fairfield, Victoria's great names from the past mark the stones and cenotaphs of century-old Ross Bay Cemetery. Victorians come here not only to leave bouquets or trace out their history in the stones, but to walk their dogs among the leafy boulevards or teach their children to ride bicycles on the level paths.

Fawn lilies carpet the quiet corners of Beacon Hill Park in springtime.

Opposite: Japanese maples show their autumn colours in Beacon Hill Park.

Peacocks live in Beacon Hill Park and at private residences around the south island. Their striking full displays are more welcome than their blood-curdling shrieks.

Opposite top: Craigdarroch Castle was built by coal baron Robert Dunsmuir for his wife, Joan.

A mere six blocks north of the castle, across Fort, Yates and Pandora streets—as well as an imaginary set of railway tracks dividing the wealthy from the humble—the district of Fernwood sits atop a long gradual rise from the Inner Harbour. A hundred years ago some of Victoria's most gracious homes were here, but eventually many became boarding houses, were divided into apartments or were torn down to make way for modest bungalows in this slightly down-at-the-heels inner-city neighbourhood. Now perhaps the liveliest and most community-minded of Victoria's core residential areas, Fernwood works hard to smooth its remaining rough edges with the presence of flourishing art galleries, crafts workshops, a kilt maker, theatre companies and cafés eminently suitable for whiling away an afternoon or evening.

The Belfry Theatre started in 1976, renting and later buying and restoring a disused church in Fernwood, and now presents up to a dozen contemporary productions a year. The alternative Theatre Inconnu, a decades-long labour of love by actor and artistic director Clayton Jevne, performs in the heavily used Fernwood Community Association space across from the Belfry. The theatres and other arts enterprises have become the heart of Fernwood, which has sprung into vibrant new life around Belfry Square and Fernwood Road. All day and well into the evening, people meet for conversation, coffee or a meal under the square's leafy shade trees.

Victoria's first water supply rose in natural springs at Spring Ridge, just west of Fernwood, but was soon replaced by water delivered by pipeline from Elk Lake.

Camas plants bloom in the Garry oak ecosystem at Government House.

Victoria West, on the far side of the Upper Harbour next to Esquimalt, has come a long way in the last 30 years, from a crumbling industrial area surrounded by small wooden houses, many of them at least 70 years old. Now some of Victoria's priciest new residential housing has sprung up as multi-storey condos in the Songhees neighbourhood. Their proximity to downtown and the magnificent views—of the Inner Harbour, Esquimalt, the Olympic Peninsula and the Sooke Hills—make them attractive to young urbanites. Newer complexes in Vic West, including Dock-side Green and the funky Railyards, are intensively ecofriendly and meet the high LEED (Leadership in Energy and Environmental Design) standards that Victoria residents seek. Even the City of Victoria is going green in a big way. The most visible sign of this is city vehicles with green-coloured tires containing no dangerous hydrocarbons, but the city is also adding recycling and composting facilities, LED traffic lights, biofuel for its trucks, more bike parking and new bike lanes to meet resident needs.

Working Victoria has traditionally centred on the inner city, especially the areas north of Fisgard Street and east of the Gorge. Residents of the area have a long history of involvement with the industry and labour that built the city, the government precinct and the region's economy of

Santa Claus rides a scooter in a mild Victoria winter.

resource exploitation and maritime trade. Many of the early immigrants to BC from England, Wales and Scotland who came to work in the coal mines and forests had cut their teeth on 19th-century British labour struggles. As shipbuilding and other manufacturing has gradually left the island, the capital region's unionized labour jobs have dwindled; most organized workers today are employed in various levels of government, health care and other public services. The working people of Victoria, like their counterparts on the mainland, still strive for child care, living wages—BC has Canada's lowest minimum wage—and safe, fair working conditions.

Paradise inevitably has its price. Housing is expensive in Victoria and its region and relatively unaffected by economic downturns that pull the rug out from under other housing markets. While the market does slump occasionally, it recovers quickly, and bargains are rare. Rental accommodation can be equally pricey and hard to find; the vacancy rate runs around 0.5 percent, much lower than the national average of 2.6 percent. Some non-residents maintain second homes here for a planned move or retirement, but rather than being rented out, many are left empty or used only occasionally.

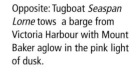

Opposite: Tugboat *Seaspan Lorne* tows a barge from Victoria Harbour with Mount Baker aglow in the pink light of dusk.

Jobs can be scarce as well, hotly contested and often less well-paid than equivalent work in other parts of the country, simply because so many people want to live here. Victoria is British Columbia's capital, so it's not surprising that the region's single largest employer is the provincial government, followed by health authorities, the armed forces, hospitals and educational institutions; private business and industry are lower on the list. Many young people leave to work in their chosen fields elsewhere, biding their time—perhaps not consciously—until they can return. Newcomers can find it challenging to make friends, too. In a bank lineup, the friendly soul who readily strikes up a conversation may just have moved here from Saskatoon; the native Victorian is likely the person texting on a phone or nose-deep in a book.

The British Columbia coat of arms in stained glass at the Parliament Buildings. The motto means "Splendour without setting," but wags have translated it as "Splendour without occasion."

People often come to Victoria for an afternoon or a few days and stay a lifetime. Some leave disappointed. Perhaps they never ventured past the few downtown shops designed to sieve modern-day gold dust from visitors' pockets, or perhaps they never managed to thaw that undeniably chilly Victoria reception to newcomers. And while this may be a gem of a city, it is a small gem that lacks some amenities of larger centres. But others quickly see past the illusion of a pale, smug, dull Victoria that tourism promoters of the 1950s touted to their more conservative guests. The city has also been keenly tuned to its human, labour and environmental rights for nearly 150 years and can claim—despite some dreadful lapses—a long, solid history of ethnic and religious diversity, inclusion and tolerance. Remember, the first Victorians—the Songhees people and the first newcomers—spoke a score of languages yet somehow managed to put their ideas across and mostly get along as neighbours.

"The situation is not faultless or so completely suited to our purposes as it might be, but I despair of any better being found on this coast," James Douglas wrote in 1842, "as I am confident that there is no other sea port north of the Columbia where so many advantages will be found combined."

Esquimalt: Commanding the Western Approaches

History crowds the narrow streets

Right: A Dall's
porpoise races ahead
of the bow of a ship.

Previous pages:
Esquimalt has been a
naval base since the
days of sail and the
Royal Navy.

Esquimalt extends
southwestward
toward Fort Rodd
Hill and Fisgard
Lighthouse on the
West Shore.

and sheltered coves of Esquimalt, and this is famously the long-time home of the Canadian Navy's Pacific Fleet. Its neighbourhoods and green spaces can claim some of the most heart-stoppingly spectacular scenery found anywhere. Esquimalt may be smaller and less well-heeled that some municipalities, but it's rich in other important ways.

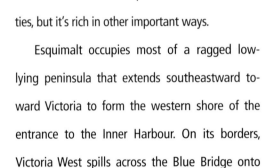

Esquimalt occupies most of a ragged low-lying peninsula that extends southeastward toward Victoria to form the western shore of the entrance to the Inner Harbour. On its borders, Victoria West spills across the Blue Bridge onto the southeastern tip of the Esquimalt Peninsula, and View Royal, a West Shore community, spreads onto the northwest isthmus. Esquimalt's seven square kilometres (2.7 square miles), almost completely bounded by the tidal Gorge Waterway and the sea, housed about 17,700 people in 2009, and that number is expected to double over the next 20 years.

Storms often batter the exposed southern shores at Macaulay Point and Saxe Point, but overall Esquimalt shares the south island's sunny, warm summers and mild, wet winters.

Water on every side, including a major deepwater harbour, means that Esquimalt looks to the sea even more than the other south-island communities. Kayakers, rowers and dragon boaters naturally gravitate to the protected waters of the Inner Harbour and the Gorge, and sailors test their mettle in the strong offshore winds.

First Peoples have known the area's advantages for thousands of years, and early newcomers quickly appreciated the harbour and surrounding lands. The first European to record a visit here was Spanish naval officer Manuel Quimper, who surveyed Juan de Fuca Strait in 1790. Landing at Albert Head, he claimed the land for Spain and gave the name Puerto de Cordova to Esquimalt Harbour, but the 1794 Nootka Convention limited Spanish activities on the West Coast. Half a century later, Britain granted rights to the island to the expanding Hudson's Bay Company. Chief Factor James Douglas acknowledged the traditional name of Is-whoy-malth, which in Northern Straits Salish means "place of gradually shoaling water."

"It is one of the better Harbours on the Coast, being perfectly safe and of easy Access, but in other respects it possesses no Attractions. Its appearance is strikingly unprepossessing, the outline of the country exhibiting a confused Assemblage of Rock and Wood," James Douglas wrote of Esquimalt during his 1842 survey of possible locations for a new HBC fur-trading fort. Esquimalt lacked the plentiful fresh water and farmable land that a fort needed, and Douglas declined the area—along with Sooke, Metchosin and Pedder Bay—in favour of Camosun, soon to be rebranded as Victoria.

Despite his generally keen eye, Douglas missed the mark with "unprepossessing." He couldn't have guessed that a century and a half later some of Esquimalt's greatest attractions would include views of Victoria's Inner Harbour, kilometres of walking and cycling paths overlooking the ever-changing waters of Juan de Fuca Strait and hectares of beaches and parks. As a place to live, work or play, Esquimalt has long been the south island's best-kept secret.

Since the Beginning

Some First Peoples' sites—of homes, fortifications and industries—have been in continuous use from about 4,000 years ago to the present day. Esquimalt lies within the traditional territory of the Lekwungen people, who spoke a dialect of the Northern Straits Salish language and once inhabited the area from Parry Bay near Metchosin all the way around to Cordova Bay on the Saanich Peninsula. James Douglas settled treaties with the Lekwungen people in 1850, and two Lekwungen-speaking groups, the Esquimalt First Nation and the Songhees First Nation, have reserves just north of Esquimalt in neighbouring View Royal.

Visiting paddlers from the Tribal Journeys canoe regatta await ceremonial greeting on the beach of Songhees Reserve.

Artifacts and archeological sites reveal the sophisticated technology and aesthetic sensibility of these people, even 3,000 years ago, though perishable materials such as wood and plant fibres haven't always survived to tell the full story. Carved stone and bone tools, weapons and ornaments show the skills of their makers, but there is also great beauty in items such as a weaving comb carved in the shape of an animal, a stone bowl in the shape of a sitting man and a set of precious copper beads. Nineteen fortified sites identified so far in the region show that life could be perilous, but during peaceful times the plentiful natural resources supported a complex society. Early resi-

A Kwakwaka'wakw bumblebee dancer performs in the Songhees bighouse.

dents raised dogs for hunting and wool, wove baskets and blankets, tanned hides, wore jewellery and may have painted their skin for beauty or ritual purposes.

Newcomers admired the Lekwungen people's fine baskets, their ornate dance costumes and their graceful canoes, each carved from a single cedar tree, that glided over the waters of the harbours, coves and inland waterways. The Lekwungen people were eager to trade and to sell their labour for construction, but the bargain proved disastrous when they contracted smallpox, a European disease to which they had no resistance.

Today the Esquimalt and Songhees bands take part in the North American Indigenous Games, held in Victoria in 1997 and every few years in other communities continent-wide, and the annual Tribal Journeys by traditional canoe that are meant to strengthen Native spirituality and promote community and personal healing. Lekwungen groups paddled to the Quinault Nation in Washington state in 2002 and to Quw'utsun (Cowichan) in 2008.

On Rocky Ground

James Douglas saw little agricultural potential in Esquimalt, but by the 1850s the Puget Sound Agricultural Company—a HBC subsidiary—had started several large farms in the area. Viewfield Farm, Esquimalt Farm and Constance Cove Farm were in Esquimalt, and Craigflower Farm was in what is now View Royal. All were meant to supply food to Fort Victoria and other nearby HBC forts, and even up-coast to Russian Alaska, but the rocky land was hard to clear of its heavy timber, and within a decade the HBC closed several farms. Viewfield and Constance Cove farms left little trace, though later footpaths, roads and municipal boundaries have followed their property lines.

The Royal Navy quickly noted the value of Esquimalt Harbour. Lieutenant James Wood of the brig *Pandora* started the first hydrographic survey in 1846, with 14 young midshipmen of the

Sailing ships at anchor in Esquimalt Harbour, circa 1868. By this time, Esquimalt served, along with Valparaiso, Chile, as the headquarters of the Royal Navy's Pacific Station. Image B-00822 courtesy of Royal BC Museum, BC Archives

St. Paul's Anglican Church on Esquimalt Road is the province's oldest surviving church still in use today.

frigate *Fisgard* and their instructor. In 1848 the British man of war HMS *Constance* became the first Royal Navy ship based at Esquimalt. By the mid-1850s Russia was trouncing Britain and France in the North Pacific naval battles of the Crimean War; the crew at Esquimalt was unable to treat the wounded, who had to be taken south to California. Expecting further casualties, the Royal Navy asked James Douglas to build a medical facility. The three wooden "Crimean huts" on three hectares (seven acres) of land at Duntze Head never saw use as hospital wards but marked Esquimalt's first naval shore establishment.

The huts are long since gone, but you can spend a fascinating day at the CFB Esquimalt Naval and Military Museum in a restored early hospital building. The naval base also has occasional open houses and special events worth watching for, including a Christmas light extravaganza that festoons ships, shore buildings and anything else that's not in motion at the time.

Not far outside the naval base is BC's oldest surviving church still in use today. St. Paul's Anglican Church was built in 1866 near Signal Hill, which is now inside CFB Esquimalt, but was moved on rollers in 1904 to Esquimalt Road. Several services are conducted there every week, offering an opportunity to see the church's heritage organ, stained glass, historic colours and plaques.

Gold seekers from all over the world flooded the south island heading for the Fraser River in 1858 and Barkerville in 1862. Hundreds, then thousands, of men arrived from California, and the larger ships used Esquimalt Harbour. Esquimalt would never again be a sleepy street or two of civilian businesses serving the small naval station; it quickly sprouted hotels, saloons and general merchants to profit from the '58ers. The track that Royal Navy sailors had hacked out of the wilderness in 1852—the forerunner of Old Esquimalt Road—became a muddy wallow as experienced miners, well-heeled hopefuls and lawless ruffians made their way to the growing tent town in Victoria before heading for the mainland.

Lieutenant Richard Mayne of the naval survey ship the *Plumper* wrote of the heavy pedestrian and vehicular traffic and the gold-mad "strangers of every tongue and country, in every variety of attire."

He added, "Vancouver Island itself is most beautiful, but turned quite upside down by the gold discovery, a regular San Francisco in 49. Yet you are hardly safe without arms & even with them, when you have to walk along paths across which gentlemen with a brace of revolvers each are settling their differences: the whiz of revolver bullets round you goes on all day & night…"

The more than 20,000 gold seekers hugely outnumbered the region's aboriginal population and few hundred settlers, and the Royal Navy anchored ships outside Esquimalt Harbour to protect British subjects from the new arrivals. Later, Russian and American expansion on the coast seemed likely, so the navy continued to increase its presence at Esquimalt.

In 1859 the Pig War—the only casualty was a black British boar on San Juan Island— broke out between Britain and the United States over possession of the Gulf Islands and the San Juan Islands. Three British warships and US infantry forces looked down each other's cannon barrels for a tense few weeks before Kaiser Wilhelm I agreed to mediate the border decision, and the Pig War ended with no shots fired in anger. The decision gave the San Juan Islands to the USA and the Gulf Islands to Britain.

Two Navies

Most Esquimalt history inevitably has a naval component. In 1865 the maintenance and supply facilities at Esquimalt served, along with Valparaiso, Chile, as the headquarters of the Royal Navy's Pacific Station. As steamships increasingly replaced sailing ships, Esquimalt became more attractive: the development of coal mines up-island at Nanaimo and later at Cumberland meant that ships could refuel with Vancouver Island coal.

Over the next few decades, the navy built a series of wooden and red brick buildings to house various services. Naden, as the shore establishment was called, soon swallowed the muddy streets and small private buildings of Old Esquimalt Village. Wharf Street, later called Pioneer Street to avoid confusion with the Victoria street, ran south from the harbour and attracted homes and businesses.

The naval dockyard was completed in 1887, enabling the Royal Navy to repair and refit ships on the West Coast. The Royal Navy turned over the defence of the West Coast to Canada in 1906, leaving only the sloop HMS *Shearwater* and the survey vessel HMS *Egeria* at Esquimalt. It was 1910 before Ottawa got around to forming the Canadian Navy; the small cruisers *Niobe* and *Rainbow*, bought from Britain, became the western fleet. So lax did BC consider the Canadian defence against marauding German warships during World War I that Premier Richard McBride bought the province its own fleet—two submarines originally destined for the Chilean Navy and spirited out of their Seattle shipyard under cover of night. Once the screams of rage died down in Ottawa, BC turned over the submarines to the fledgling Canadian Navy.

People from all over Canada discover Esquimalt when they serve in the navy, and a significant number later return there to live. For over 160 years, Naden has been the heart of Esquimalt—but not its whole body.

"Esquimalt is unique," said former mayor Chris Clement. "I can't think of another community where you have the possibility of all the civic facilities and services being within a two-block area."

Civilian community life in Esquimalt revolves around the compact precinct on Esquimalt Road that embraces the municipal hall, library, park, recreation centre, sports complex and shopping mall. The many different types of people who frequent this hub keep the place buzzing. The library

Opposite: Shipyard workers are dwarfed by the size of the hull that they're power washing.

has expanded several times over the years, and the municipal offices have moved into a new building. But Esquimalt, like neighbouring Saanich, is in search of a village core. Intensive planning and consultation with residents over several years has evolved ideas for a mixed-use centre with civic and residential buildings clustered around a pleasant town square and a family-oriented "high street" shopping district.

Celebration is one of Esquimalt's strengths, perhaps in the naval spirit of greeting safely returned ships and sailors. The biggest annual civilian celebration takes a lighthearted broadside at the naval presence with a pirate theme. One of the more startling aspects of Buccaneer Days every June is the presence of Canadian Navy personnel sporting eye patches and cutlasses. Generations of Esquimalt kids might grow up thinking the officers and ratings are pirates in their spare time—if they weren't having too much fun to notice the incongruity. Highlights of the weekend include a piratical parade, dances for teens and adults, a pirate's den for children, arts and crafts, rugby and lacrosse games, model railroad demonstrations and mountains of food. The Victoria Harbour Ferry Company lays on a special Buccaneer Express Ferry from the Inner Harbour across to West Bay in Esquimalt, where buses carry visiting mateys to the festivities.

Breezes that comb the shoreline wildflowers at Macaulay Park blow in across Juan de Fuca Strait from the open Pacific.

Parks and Paths

Walking, picnicking and admiring the scenery are only minutes away from anywhere in Esquimalt, which claims proportionately more green space than any other municipality in the region, with 40 hectares (108 acres) of parks, beaches, walking paths, sports fields and natural areas.

Some of the parks and paths hug the shoreline, with many sitting and picnicking spots. And there are many interesting sites off the beaten path, unknown to non-residents. For instance, walking through the forest paths of Saxe Point Park down to the rocky shore, you can admire the unequalled view east toward James Bay and Beacon Hill Park in Victoria and south toward the snowy peaks of the Olympic Peninsula in Washington state. Continuing eastward, past small well-kept houses with gardens that show meticulous care, you'll pass the Fleming Park boat launch and cross into Macaulay Point Park.

The Gorge Waterway comes to mind immediately when people think of Esquimalt's natural beauty, although four different communities—Esquimalt, Victoria, Saanich and the West Shore's View Royal—have jurisdiction over the watercourse. Teeming with fish and waterfowl, rich in plant life and navigable for kilometres from the sea to the upper end of Portage Inlet, the Gorge was a larder and a highway for First Peoples. As well as fishing and hunting there, in stormy weather

The Selkirk Trestle offers a scenic walk across the Gorge Waterway.

Mute swans and many migratory birds visit Esquimalt Lagoon.

Once home to gold rush magistrate and commissioner Peter O'Reilly, Point Ellice House is now open to the public for tea.

they used the Gorge as a safe, sheltered route from Victoria Harbour to Esquimalt Harbour, with one short portage at the upper end.

The tidal race at the Gorge Narrows helped to persuade James Douglas to build a HBC fort on the Inner Harbour; on his first survey, he wrote of plans to build a watermill there to harness its energy for light industry. Craigflower Farm transported its produce along the Gorge to Fort Victoria. Light industry, much of it marine in nature, occupied the shoreline from the Inner Harbour up past the Point Ellice Bridge; the full-service Point Hope Shipyard has carried out business since 1873 on the Upper Harbour. Some of the earliest great homes of Victoria, including magistrate and gold commissioner Peter O'Reilly's Point Ellice House, overlooked the Gorge or its lower reach, Selkirk Water.

A generation later, in a region transformed by gold rushes, epidemics and wars, the Gorge became the city's favourite recreation spot. It boasted annual regattas, a swimming pool, a Japanese tea garden and a large park above the Tillicum Bridge. BC Electric opened an amusement park in 1905 and the 0.4-hectare (one-acre) Takata Gardens, designed by Isaburo Kishida (who also designed the Japanese gardens at Hatley Park and the Butchart Gardens) in 1907. Many courtships and friendships blossomed among the pavilions and sedate promenades, a popular destination for genteel society outings—and, scandalously, for prostitutes displaying their charms. The gardens and tearoom operated until World War II, when the Takata family was relocated to an internment camp, and vandals ruined the gardens. Today, near the site of the old Takata Gardens, a striking wooden Japanese gate frames a remarkable view of the Gorge Narrows from one side and from the other side

a monumental Japanese stone lantern. A small Japanese garden with replanted Japanese plum trees, an arched bridge and ponds restores the beauty and peace of the historic setting.

People built houses and businesses outward along the Gorge banks between the two world wars, and the shipbuilding industry went into overdrive during World War II. By the 1960s apartments and houses lined even the wilder reaches of Portage Inlet, and storm drains and sewage quickly degraded the waterway. By the 1980s, when shipbuilding had dwindled and most homes were on the sewer system, water quality started to improve. But most of the great stands of Douglas fir, Garry oak and arbutus were gone, and pollution made the water unswimmable and devoid of wildlife. In 1990 concerned residents formed the Gorge Waterway Action Society to study whether the Gorge could be restored and what activities it should support. Volunteers put in thousands of hours on cleanup and restoration projects, and their work has paid off.

Today, with pollution coming under control and wildlife returning, the Gorge is again a beautiful and cherished area. Gorge-front homes in Saanich, Esquimalt and Victoria are much sought after and increasingly costly, but anyone can enjoy the public green space on both banks of the waterway. On the Esquimalt bank just above Tillicum Bridge a riverside path leads through Esquimalt Gorge Park to a lookout above the rushing, eddying waters of Gorge Narrows, where the reversing waterfall once flowed.

Every day many people walk the well-kept pathways, picnic with their families, watch otters, herons, mink and other animals along the banks, or enjoy the waterway afloat. Where the manicured parks and paths leave the shoreline, native plants quickly return to create pockets of wilderness best seen from the water. The Victoria Canoe and Kayak Club, which occupies a historic building above the Tillicum Bridge, offers lessons, guided tours and recreational outings year-round.

Relatively few cities offer a chance to live, work, play and travel along a winding natural waterway of constantly changing beauty. Salt water and sweetwater mingle and flow in the Gorge. Where there is moving water, there is life; where there is life, there is change. Trees and wildflowers blossom in spring, flourish in summer and fade into fall. A variety of wild creatures quietly visit the banks, and every day brings shifting patterns of light and reflection.

Victoria Canoe and Kayak Club occupies an ideal location on the Gorge Waterway.

Dragon boat crews practise on the relatively calm Gorge Waterway.

"Nautical kitsch" decorates a house across from the Princess Mary Restaurant in Esquimalt.

Walks in Esquimalt

One of the most exciting recent developments for Esquimalt and its neighbouring municipalities is the E&N Rail Trail project, a multi-use pathway running parallel to the railway tracks and within its right-of-way from Victoria through Esquimalt to View Royal and Langford, where it will eventually join the Trans Canada Trail. Stage One is scheduled for completion in the winter of 2010, with later stages to follow.

The West Bay Walkway, also called West Song Way, is a five-kilometre (three-mile) path and boardwalk that follows the seashore from eastern Esquimalt to downtown Victoria. A minor detour through small streets at the Esquimalt end will take you among historic and unusual buildings, including a house at 464 Head Street decorated by the late John Keziere. Pirates and mermaids sprout from the windows, gables and roof in a style that Esquimalt historian Sherri K. Robinson calls "nautical kitsch."

A stroll along West Bay Walkway follows the seashore from eastern Esquimalt to downtown Victoria.

Across the street is the newest incarnation of Victoria's beloved seafood restaurant, the Princess Mary. It once occupied a Canadian Pacific Princess-class steamer that had been scrapped after long service and dragged up onto Harbour Road in Victoria West; its new digs overlook West Bay Marina and are full of memorabilia of CP ships, naval vessels and other maritime history. In the hands of owner and chef Bill Lang, the seafood is as good as ever.

Esquimalt's best-known inn for decades was the Old England Inn on Lampson Street, owned for years by Sam and Rosina Lane, English immigrants who were tireless promoters of Victoria and partially responsible for the "little bit of old England" flavour of Victoria's post–World War II tourist industry. The large 1906 Tudor revival home was designed by Victoria's second most famous architect, Samuel McClure. (The most famous, Francis Rattenbury, was murdered by his chauffeur, his second wife's lover.) Now called the English Inn, it regularly hosts weddings and honeymoons in its gardens and the Rosemeade Bistro restaurant.

Surprisingly, many guidebooks and websites about the Victoria region don't mention Esquimalt, where historically incomes have been lower and the economy thinner than in neighbouring municipalities. Yet the area has taken off in the last few years as a prime place to live, where small older houses (many of them beautifully restored or updated), high-design floathomes and top-end condos with panoramic views can be had for relatively lower cost than elsewhere. There are also multi-million-dollar waterfront and view homes to rival anything on the south island. And you can't beat the commute. Getting from Esquimalt's town hall to downtown Victoria is only about a half-hour walk, 15-minute cycle or 10-minute drive past beaches, parks and heritage buildings—unless you prefer to travel by harbour ferry or kayak. For people who work downtown but want to live economically in a spectacular setting, Esquimalt is a happy choice.

Oak Bay: Pheasant Under Glass

You could be strolling the high street

of a small, tidy English town a few generations ago, one lined with half-timbered Tudor-style buildings that house gift shops, antique shops, book shops, a tea importer, a greengrocer, bakeries, delicatessens and pretty tea rooms. Trundling across the street with magnificent disregard for traffic bylaws are older gentlemen in quality tweeds, often patched, and ladies in attire ranging from rummage sale to haute couture. You're not dreaming—this is still western Canada—but you are in deepest Oak Bay, "behind the Tweed Curtain."

Right: Tulips surround a house in Oak Bay.

Previous pages: Oak Bay Marina is home port for casual day sailors and round-the-world yachtsmen.

King George Terrace rises over a rock outcrop overlooking Harling Point.

But there's more to Oak Bay than nostalgia for a vanished Edwardian past. You might just as easily see software developers bearing takeout coffees heading back to the office to hunch over their keyboards, extras dressed to kill for the local film industry or volunteers marching off to fight invasive plant species in Uplands Park. Flocks of neon-garbed cyclists on titanium frames coast along the narrow streets, sharing the roadways with many pedestrians and a noticeable proportion of electric and hybrid cars.

Still, "charming," "genteel" and "more English than the English" are the words we tend to hear when locals discuss Oak Bay, often in the bemused tones reserved for dotty aunts with too many cats. Oak Bay is the most "Victorian" of Greater Victoria's regions, and visitors and newcomers swarm to its shops and restaurants like bees to honey. Other folk might huff that Oak Bay is unbearably smug, but most would concede that Oak Bay has rather a lot to be smug about.

An Oak Bay council in the 1970s, blocking a large development scheme, announced, "Oak Bay residents enjoy a unique lifestyle. We are not overly impressed by concrete and chrome. We are not overly concerned that grass and flowers sometimes grow through the cracks in the sidewalks. We like things the way they are now." In other words, by contemplating and conserving their own traditional values—at a time when other BC politicians were calling air pollution "the smell of success"—Oak Bay quietly led the way toward a saner, more ecofriendly world. Today its approximately 18,000 residents inhabit a modest area of 10.4 square kilometres (four square miles)—two-thirds the size of Victoria proper and one-eighth the size of Saanich—that even after a century and a half of development has retained its striking beauty.

Oak Bay's lush oak meadows starred with blue camas and other wildflowers, which delighted early travellers, were not natural grassland, as once believed, but created by First Peoples' regular burning of the underbrush. At one time these meadows may have stretched from the West Shore right around to the Saanich Peninsula. Victoria and its municipalities have swallowed most of the original forests and grasslands over the past century, and residents now struggle to protect small pockets of natural beauty. But Oak Bay preserves an afterimage of the original landscape of the south island; gnarled oaks and drifts of camas grow happily among its residential areas and in its peaceful, sunny parks.

The island's bones show clearly in Oak Bay's gouged and polished rock outcrops, which rise from the otherwise gently rolling terrain of soil over layers of clay. Granite boulders lie scattered

Trillium and Oregon grape thrive in shady spots.

The heritage Gonzales Observatory offers a superb panoramic view of Juan de Fuca Strait. A weather station operated here from 1914 for 75 years.

Willows Beach hosts the Oak Bay Tea Party every June, but between major events it's a relaxing place to picnic on the beach or just enjoy the sun and sand.

A paddle-boarder explores the shallows at Willows Beach.

throughout the area, signs of the south island's once heavily glaciated landscape. Seashore rocks at Cattle Point, for example, bear deep grooves where vast glaciers a kilometre (about half a mile) deep ground boulders and gravel across their surface about 14,000 years ago. As the glaciers melted, a rush of grit-laden meltwater carved winding cavities in the rock. "These torrents sand-blasted the serpentine channels seen here and there on exposed rock. They coil this way and that, sinuous and ever-changing, sometimes at right angles to adjacent north-south grooves," wrote William Stavdal in 1976 in *Monday Magazine*, adding that some of the finest examples can be seen on the beach below the Chinese Cemetery at Harling Point.

Native plant species returning to the area after the glacier receded took many years to lay down the topsoil that supports today's flora: thickets of willow, native plum and cherry, snowberry, Oregon grape and wild rose; groves of Douglas fir, arbutus, oak, cedar and maple; and delicate drifts of wildflowers. People quickly learn to sit cautiously on rock outcrops colonized by small native cacti.

Exotic plants are another matter. As early as the 1850s Oak Bay residents were planting boulevards and gardens of trees, shrubs and flowers from "the old country" to remind them of the homes they'd left behind forever. "Old China hands" and others who retired here from diplomatic or military service in far corners of the world imported their favourite deodars, monkey-puzzle trees and ginkgos. Then there are the palm trees. Palms are not native to the region, but you'd never guess that in Oak Bay, where they're so popular in residential gardens that the municipality hosts an annual sale of young palm trees.

People here cherish the palms as an unstated demonstration of the region's gentle climate, at its mildest in Oak Bay with its sunny eastward and southward prospects. On average, 583 millimetres (22.93 inches) of rain fall annually in the area, with average high and low temperatures of 14°C (57°F) and 7°C (45°F) and 2,193 hours of bright sunshine.

Almost as much as they love the climate and landscape, Oak Bay people love a party. Willows Beach is the scene of the annual Oak Bay Tea Party in June, a madcap Alice-in-Wonderland-style celebration. The party kicks off with the Mad Hatter's Fun Run, in which serious runners and a swarm of parents with baby buggies and strollers jog around the municipality. A parade follows. Local aerobatics and military pilots take part in an air show and fly-past that can feature some of the south island's restored vintage planes. Food, bathtub races, kayak rides, carnival rides, competitions, live entertainment and a dance keep tea partiers busy till evening.

In the mayor's tea-cup race off Willows Beach, now a fixture, the Oak Bay mayor traditionally challenges another south island celebrity to arrive first at the finish line. In tippy fibreglass teacups propelled by mismatched oars, this is no easy feat; dunking and retrieval by the Oak Bay Sea Rescue boat are all part of the fun. Past opponents have included the mayors of Victoria and Saanich, David Hahn, the president of BC Ferries, and Olympic rower Silken Laumann. The Oak Bay Tea Party provides ample opportunities for residents to have some fun with their tweedy image. Intended as a one-time event in 1963, sponsored by the Oak Bay Bored of Trade (Kiwanis Club), the tea party now takes place annually and draws both local people and visitors.

Wealth of the Land

The mild climate and gentle landscape of the Oak Bay area richly supported several groups of First Peoples in villages and fortified sites before Europeans arrived. The annual harvest and hunting cycle generously provided for people's needs. As in other parts of the region, carefully maintained oak meadows provided camas bulbs to roast in summer, and thickets yielded willow and other materials for weaving baskets and mats. Hunters brought ducks, deer and other animals from the woods, and inshore waters and beaches teemed with fish and shellfish.

Many shops still proudly occupy half-timbered Tudor-style buildings on Oak Bay Avenue.

Many artifacts, graves and building foundations have come to light throughout Oak Bay, and the Lekwungen (Songhees) people also carry the knowledge of their ancient uses and have traditional names for the locations. Chikawich (McNeill Bay or Shoal Bay)—the word means "big hips" and describes how the houses were laid out—was the home of four aboriginal groups, including the Chekwungeen people. Sahsima, meaning "harpoon," was the name for Harling Point, where Haylas the Creator wielded his great power to turn a seal harpooner to stone; today the Chinese Cemetery, the oldest in Canada and a national historic site, occupies part of the point. Sitchanalth (today's Willows Beach, a favourite Oak Bay park nestled between Cattle Point and Turkey Head) describes a place where sand engulfed trees and drift logs; it was a major village.

During the smallpox epidemic of 1862, people returned to their traditional territory on Discovery Island (called Tichless, meaning "island"), which is visible about three kilometres (two miles) offshore from Willows Beach. At Sungayka, or "snow patches" (Cadboro Bay), residents kept a watch for northern raiders from a headland fortress near the present-day Royal Victoria Yacht Club.

At low tide, people would play qoqwialls on the exposed sandy beach. Six extended-family households lived at Sungayka, near present-day Gyro Park, when the Hudson's Bay Company founded Uplands Farm in the late 1840s, and occasionally there was friction between newcomers and long-time aboriginal residents.

A recent archeological dig at Turkey Head near the Oak Bay Marina—its traditional name of Shpwhung means "flying dust" or "fog"—produced many tools, especially ones for woodworking. The excavation was especially important because archeologists from Camosun College collaborated on it with the Songhees First Nation, which owns the finds and uses them to teach about Songhees culture.

Today the Lekwungen people have reserves on Chatham Island and Discovery Island, but no one is in permanent residence. Beaching or coming ashore on reserve lands in BC requires written permission from the appropriate First Nation. Apart from occasional use of these islands, Oak Bay's aboriginal population consists of individuals who choose to live in its sunny southern neighbourhoods.

Home from Home

The first newcomers to leave the shelter of the Hudson's Bay Company fort in the late 1840s knew a good thing when they saw it. Their hunting parties and picnics among the oak meadows to the east and south of Fort Victoria brought back fond memories of the open English countryside. All of the land east of the fort was set aside for fur trading and farming to produce supplies for Victoria and other forts. However, the HBC soon sold off parcels of the Oak Bay wilderness to landowners associated with the company, as vast waterfront estates.

The HBC's own Uplands Farm, at the site of today's Royal Victoria Yacht Club in northern Oak Bay, was its largest farm at 452.4 arable hectares (1,118 acres). It stretched roughly from Cadboro Bay south to Cattle Point. The farm featured Oak Bay's first non-aboriginal structures: a wharf, livestock barns and housing for the superintendent and about 17 workers. The first trail from the fort to the farm laid down the route of today's Fort Street and Oak Bay's oldest road, Cadboro Bay Road. Uplands and Cattle Point parks now occupy the southeastern corner of the old farm site.

John Tod, the chief trader at Fort Victoria, built Oak Bay's first private home on his parcel south of Uplands Farm and which included much of the Oak Bay waterfront. Oak Bay House, now a heritage site at 2564 Heron Street, usually called John Tod House, is the oldest continuously inhabited surviving house in western Canada. Tod wrote to a friend in England, perhaps of this location, "from my new home, I have wonderful views of the sea and mountains in all directions." Tod and his Métis wife Sophia Lolo—the last of his four wives—lived in Oak Bay until his death in 1882. The house had a reputation for being haunted by a Native woman until around 1952, when the owner uncovered the remains of an Asian or aboriginal woman buried more than two metres (6.5 feet) deep; the house may have been built on the site of a First Nations burial ground. Willows Park and the Esplanade today occupy the waterfront portions of the old Tod farm.

The captain of the HBC steamship the *Beaver*, William McNeill, bought waterfront land from the company in 1850 for his homestead on Shoal Bay, now often called McNeill Bay. McNeill knew the area well; his 1837 recommendation of Camosun led to James Douglas's choice of the site for Fort Victoria. McNeill's wife Matilda was a Kaigani Haida woman from the Alaskan panhandle. By about 1860, when a photo was taken, the McNeills had built a house of peeled logs and a barn near the seashore. The Royal Victoria Golf Course now lies just east of the McNeill farm's former site.

In 1851 Joseph Despard Pemberton, the son of a lord mayor of Dublin, arrived to act as the HBC's surveyor-general and engineer. Over the years he laid out the townsite of Victoria and

Left: Oak Bay's war memorial was built in 1948 to honour the dead of World War II but now also lists casualties of other wars. Beyond the sculpture, Uplands Park preserves a rare Garry oak ecosystem.

Below: Residents on the Victoria and Oak Bay waterfront enjoy unequalled views across Juan de Fuca Strait to Washington state.

Bottom: Songhees bighouses once lined the shore of Chikawich ("big hips") or McNeill Bay, still popular with beachcombing Oak Bay residents.

Grazing sheep and cattle took over the heritage Victoria Golf Club for its first 10 years, but today golfers have priority. Trial Island, now an ecological reserve, lies offshore.

Lawn bowling remains popular in Oak Bay and Victoria.

surveyed much of Vancouver Island, and in his travels he admired Oak Bay. His large parcel south of John Tod's property and north of Captain McNeill's contained spectacular rock heights and beaches, including the locations of the present-day Oak Bay village and the southern Oak Bay waterfront, but was less suitable for farming. Oak Bay's Native Plant Garden, a quiet retreat of only 0.2 hectares (about half an acre), today occupies a shady corner of the old Pemberton estate.

Isabella Ross, BC's first female landowner, bought the southernmost portion of Oak Bay, which is now part of the city of Victoria. She gave her name to Ross Bay and also named Foul Bay under its original spelling of Fowl Bay, today it's often called Gonzales Bay. Like John Tod's wives and Mrs. McNeill, Isabella was of First Nations ancestry; her husband Charles Ross had been the HBC chief factor who built Fort Victoria in 1843. On the former site of her farm, generations of children have learned to ride their bicycles among the shady lanes of Ross Bay Cemetery, which is the Victoria area's largest cemetery and the resting place of the city's most famous artists, entrepreneurs and politicians.

Eventually these five estates were divided into many smaller parcels and subdivisions, and the Oak Bay village grew up along Oak Bay Avenue. Now apartments, retail businesses, professional office space and a few remaining private homes line the avenue from Oak Bay Junction to the sea. The avenue is a walker's delight and a shopper's dream, with many small one-of-a-kind shops offering unusual imports and local crafts.

The Sporting Life

Oak Bay today has a prevailing air of tradition and heritage. Despite its fascinating evolution from wilderness and farmland to recreational spot to residential suburb, there's relatively little evidence left of its earliest buildings. Fire claimed the impressively large and visually striking exhibition hall at the Willows fairground, and the Willows racetrack and speedway are long lost to residential and commercial growth. So is Canada's first arena with artificial ice, built in 1911 "away out" on Epworth Street (then called Empress Street) at Cadboro Bay Road. The Patrick family built the arena largely to house the Victoria Senators, the local entry in the new Pacific Coast Hockey Association. The Patrick Arena hosted the first hockey game played on artificial ice in Canada in 1912 and went on to be the scene of many other hockey firsts including the introduction of the blue line, the forward pass, changing on the fly and numbers on hockey jerseys. In 1925 the Victoria Cougars, successors to the Senators, won the Stanley Cup by defeating the Montreal Canadiens in this Oak Bay arena. Four years later the grand wooden arena, with its square corner towers and arched front roof, burned to the ground, taking with it the south island's dream of becoming a hockey powerhouse in western Canada.

Windsor Park, heavily used for decades for rugby, baseball, cricket and other field sports and recreation programs, was originally called Oak Bay Park. BC Electric built the park in 1890, says Oak Bay's volunteer archivist Jean Sparks, to entice people to ride its trams to what was then a seaside resort area east of Victoria. Its counterpart west of the city was BC Electric Park on the Gorge Waterway, now Esquimalt Gorge Park.

Windsor Park was built by BC Electric to lure Victorians to ride its trams. BC Archives, D-02608

The great seaside hotels that once attracted world travellers are long gone. In 1901, when the future King George V and Queen Mary stayed at the Mount Baker Hotel near the present-day Oak Bay Marina, prominent Victoria families loaned the hotel furniture and artwork for the royal suite. An escort of Royal Marines camped in two large tents on the beach. George was a favourite in Oak Bay, and scenic King George Terrace was named in his honour. The Mount Baker burned to the ground a year after the couple's stay.

During a 1907 speaking tour of Canada Rudyard Kipling stayed in the Oak Bay Hotel, later called the Olde Charming Inn, which burned down in 1962. After an evening of drinking together, he wrote a poem for his host, John Virtue, which probably did not earn him his 1907 Nobel Prize:

A gilded mirror and a polished bar
Myriads of glasses strewn ajar
A kind-faced man all dressed in white
That's my recollection of last night

The streets were narrow and far too long
Sidewalks slippery, policemen strong
The slamming door, the sea-going hack
That's my recollection of getting back

A rickety staircase and hard to climb
But I rested often, I'd lots of time
An awkward keyhole and a misplaced chair
Informed my wife that I was there.

The English-style Oak Bay Beach Hotel, built in 1927, was the area's longest-lived hotel until the old half-timbered building was demolished to make way for a new hotel and condo complex. Luncheons and teas in its formal dining room and quiet drinks in its cozy pub, The Snug, had been long-standing Oak Bay traditions.

The only accommodation available in Oak Bay during the Oak Bay Beach Hotel's transformation, the much smaller Oak Bay Guest House is neatly placed between Windsor Park, the Oak Bay Marina and Victoria Golf Course. Oak Bay doesn't permit B&Bs, but the guest house has been in operation since 1922, and is allowed to carry on under a grandfather clause. The half-timbered English-style building and well-kept gardens appeal to visitors, but little do they know that the building

Much of Oak Bay's architectural legacy has been lost to fire, including the Oak Bay Hotel. Image F-0008 courtesy of Royal BC Museum, BC Archives

Bald eagles hunt and nest around the south island.

may have had an unsavoury past. "It has an interesting history because it has been many different things over the years. It may even have been a brothel, but we can't prove it," says Jean Sparks.

A good number of Oak Bay mansions, many of them designed by famous local architects Francis Rattenbury and Samuel McClure, retain their original grandeur. Rattenbury built his own Tudor-style home on Beach Drive for his first wife, Florence, and their two children, but later left her for a younger woman, a gifted musician. Rattenbury had the heat and water turned off and left Florence languishing in the house, outraging Victorians with this abuse. (Twelve years later, his 18-year-old chauffeur, and his second wife Alma's lover, killed Rattenbury with a wooden mallet.) The house is now the junior campus of the private Glenlyon Norfolk School.

The municipality's online walking tour map lays out several routes that pass by great houses and their gardens, and the Heritage Oak Bay website offers points of historic and architectural interest (see Resources).

Parks and Wild Places

The golden landscape that has drawn so many people to Oak Bay over the last century and a half is carefully protected through its many parks and beaches. Uplands Park preserves 30.8 hectares (76 acres) of Garry oak meadow, the island's most endangered habitat, in a pedestrian-only environment rich with birdsong and rare wild plants. Cattle Point across Beach Drive offers a smaller walking area and car access to its two boat-launch ramps. In the 1890s, when the BC Cattle Company ran stock on the Uplands Farm, barges towed close to land would release cattle to swim or wade ashore. Thirty years later, rumour insists, Cattle Point became a popular place to land contraband when Prohibition in the US rocketed BC liquor sales to huge profits. Jim Hume wrote in a 2009 *Times Colonist* article that in those years the basement of the Royal Victoria Yacht Club was sometimes piled high with cases of Scotch whisky stored by well-connected and well-organized rumrunners.

One of the region's most significant lost streams, Bowker Creek, rises from several sources, one near UVic's Faculty Club and another one in Saanich near Shelbourne Street and Mckenzie Avenue on the former site of Rosebank Farm, started in 1857 by John and Jessie Irvine. Once a year-round source of fresh drinking water for First Peoples and a spawning stream for coho and chum salmon and cutthroat trout, the creek meandered through meadows and wetlands to flow into the sea at Oak Bay. In 1958 writer C.B. Fisher described Bowker Creek in the *Daily Colonist* as "a sad sack of a creek, shorn of its beauty, slipping back to a mere trickle of polluted and frustrated water." More than half of the stream's length is now trapped in culverts or—after 1970s "beautification" programs—in rock and concrete streambeds. Volunteers are working to restore the stream and its banks, creating a greenway corridor between neighbourhoods and providing wildlife habitat. It's once again possible to walk and picnic beside the stream, for example at Fireman's Park just east of the police and fire station on Monterey Avenue.

Discovery Island was the site of a lighthouse operated by Mary Ann Croft, Canada's first female lighthouse keeper, and gained a reputation as a haven for rumrunners during Prohibition. Today no one lives permanently on the island, but an automated light still operates on Pandora Hill at the eastern end, and the northern part is a Songhees First Nation reserve. Captain E.G. Beaumont bought the southern part of the island in 1918 and lived there for more than 50 years, welcoming generations of scouts and cadets on camping trips. The self-styled "King of Discovery Island" steered his boat to and from the island through dangerous rocks and shoals. He once said, "I know where all the rocks are. I bumped into all of them and once in a while I bump into them again to remind myself of their presence." In 1972 Beaumont's land became a marine park where small-boaters and kayakers can camp.

Opposite: In this aerial view of Oak Bay, Uplands Golf Course is in the foreground with Juan de Fuca Strait and the Olympic Mountains behind.

Kohweechella ("where there are many fish") was named Mary Tod Island around 1856 by Mary's father, John Tod of the HBC. Lying half a kilometre (0.3 miles) east of the Oak Bay Marina, it was better known for many years as Jimmy Chicken Island. In the 1890s Jimmy lived in a small shack on the island with his wife Jenny, selling fish and clams to the Mount Baker Hotel. The affectionate pair were popular with local residents, notwithstanding their fondness for stealing poultry. When Jimmy died in 1901, a few years after Jenny, more than 100 canoes of Songhees people beached at Oak Bay for a ceremony to mark his passing. They later paddled his body to nearby Chatham Island

for burial beside Jenny. The small island was bequeathed by Francis Rattenbury to Oak Bay on behalf of his friend (and Rudyard Kipling's drinking mate) John Virtue, with the stipulation that no building or structure would be permitted there. The island is a short paddle from Oak Bay, and today remains a wild place where endangered plants and animals flourish and visitors can walk the natural trails and enjoy the beaches.

Walking is an Oak Bay passion rivalled only by cycling and perhaps boating. The small municipality's surprising number of parks and beaches certainly make attractive destinations.

Top: Discovery Island, once a rumrunners' haven, is now a marine park for small-boaters and kayakers.

Above: A classic sailboat off Trial Island in Oak Bay.

Just east of the Victoria boundary, for example, four parks offer breathtaking sea views on or near Harling Point, where the Chinese Cemetery was built in 1903. The Chinese Consolidated Benevolent Association bought the land for a cemetery because of its superior feng shui qualities. You needn't be an expert in Chinese building and landscape design to treasure the point's exceptional atmosphere of power and beauty. This is the place where Haylas, the Creator of Lekwungen legend, transformed the land. On a winter morning, with a breeze teasing apart the offshore fog that mutes the ocean murmur, Harling Point seems separate from the rest of the rocky shore and peacefully adrift in another time and place.

A great walk in any season takes you through the Garry oak meadows and wetlands of Uplands Park to the shoreline at Cattle Point, a popular boat launch and a favourite place for people to walk dogs. The 30.8-hectare (76-acre) park may contain the largest single tract of Garry oak woodlands in the region, though smaller pockets survive in other areas. A long list of other native plants flourish here, many of them endangered or threatened, alongside more common species.

Volunteers over the years have been weeding out invasive plants—including European hawthorn and ash, broom, gorse and English ivy—that encroach on the park's fragile habitat. In 2010 the newly formed Friends of Uplands Park group signed up 60 new volunteers to help conserve the park's endangered Garry oak meadow ecosystem.

In spring the camas, wild rose, fawn lilies, satin flowers and other wildflowers bloom fragrantly, and birds build their nests in the dense thickets of snowberry and willow that line the paths. A spring walk calls for waterproof footwear, since the paths can become mudholes after a few days of rain. Quail families scurry through the undergrowth, songbirds flit from branch to branch, and hawks and eagles circle overhead. On a summer evening, with a breeze lifting from the water, the park offers a cool, leafy haven among the arbutuses and massive oaks. In fall, you'll see wreaths and flowers left at the World War II memorial at the edge of the park on Beach Drive, where a

service is held on Remembrance Day before the statue of a grieving woman. Winter is a good time to enjoy the rocky shoreline at Cattle Point under the breaking surf and spume driven in by a stiff southeaster.

The University of Victoria campus straddles the northern edge of Oak Bay.

A Green Campus

At the northern edge of Oak Bay, where forests and wetland once gave way to strawberry farms and later an army camp, lies the University of Victoria, which started offering classes at its new campus in 1965. One half of UVic lies in Oak Bay, the other half in Saanich. Now, about 20,000 students and 5,000 faculty and staff members work in the eclectically designed buildings clustered within and around Ring Road. One of its newer buildings is the striking cedar-clad First Peoples House, a centre for aboriginal studies and student life; like many university buildings and civic buildings in the region, it embodies ecofriendly LEED (Leadership in Energy and Environmental Design) planning. Just over a tenth of the students live in on-campus residences, and 70 percent come from outside the Victoria region.

The university consistently tops national surveys for all-around excellence. The 10 faculties, crossing the spectrum from theoretical sciences to applied arts, win international honours and turn out top-flight graduates every year. So what is the most pressing topic on the minds of its staff and students? Rabbits.

An estimated 2,000 rabbits live on the campus, nibbling the greenery, cadging veggie handouts from students and leaving their calling cards on the manicured campus lawns. Every spring the maintenance staff try to trap the tame rabbits, and the *Times Colonist* runs stories about "irate rabbit activists" who protest their capture and humane euthanasia. Every spring more tiny, adorable rabbits—many, many tiny, adorable rabbits—hop into sight. All this would be entertaining, but for the fate of the rabbits. The university is evolving a humane plan for dealing with the problem.

About 25,000 students, faculty and staff study and work on the UVic Campus—which is also home to an estimated 2,000 rabbits.

Saanich and the Peninsula: Emerging | 5

On winter mornings, when fog blankets

Right: "Old Man by the Sea" is one of several sculptures by Nathan Scott commissioned by the town of Sidney. Visitors often do a double-take when they realize the person sitting at the other end of the bench is cast in bronze.

Previous pages: Early spring brings out daffodils and pickers.

There's no scrimping on the landscaping of Sidney's Beacon Avenue.

the coves and inshore waters and swirls like dancing wraiths over low-lying fields, the Saanich Peninsula seems more like an island than a long headland reaching northward from Victoria. Eventually the fog drifts offshore, and inland away from the grey winter sea, and darkly wooded heights rise from the layered mist. Always it waits, seen or unseen, this rocky spine of the peninsula, emerging from ancient days.

As rolling oak meadows and drifts of bright flowers characterized early Victoria, the Saanich Peninsula was a place of wooded heights, a broad interior plateau and kilometres of sand and shingle beaches contained by rocky points.

The last ice age reshaped this landscape of about 190 square kilometres (73 square miles) almost beyond recognition from its ancient tundra, pushing more than a kilometre of ice laden with rocks of all sizes down toward the ocean. It scoured and furrowed the bedrock and reshaped the deposits left by earlier glaciers, leaving monadnocks, or isolated hills, that resisted erosion.

A handful of these sentinels overlook the peninsula—including Mount Tolmie, Mount Douglas, Observatory Hill and Mount Newton—from elevations of 124 to 227 metres (406.8 to 744.8 feet). Today Mount Douglas and Mount Tolmie usually buzz with hikers, naturalists, mountain bikers and visitors viewing the region sprawled below.

The ice sheet also left deep deposits of boulders, gravel, sand and silt on the peninsula's central plateau. Some of the area's earliest industries exploited the glacial moraines to extract sand and gravel. This glacial till contained the remains of ice-age animals that once roamed the cool plains of western Canada at least 10,000 years ago, when sea levels were lower and this area was still connected to BC's mainland. Mastodons, mammoths, early horses and ice-age bison and musk-oxen all left evidence, mostly bone or ivory fragments. When sea levels rose, they wiped out any trace of early aboriginal settlements along the coastline.

The central plateau is all that some visitors see of the peninsula as they rush south toward Victoria on the Patricia Bay Highway (Highway 17) from the airport or ferry terminals; unknowingly, they're skirting some of the south island's most intriguing history and geography.

The Pat Bay, with perfect island logic, ventures nowhere near its namesake Patricia Bay, which fronts on Saanich Inlet on the western side of the peninsula. Instead the highway hugs the eastern shore, often in sight of the Gulf Islands and the US San Juan Islands across Haro Strait. The four-lane highway starts at Swartz Bay at the northern tip of the Saanich Peninsula, once a quiet cove where a tiny Gulf Islands ferry docked and now home to a large BC Ferries complex handling traffic to the islands and BC's mainland. The highway hits its stride alongside hayfields and cattle pastures and a less-than-beautiful stretch of commercial sites.

The Pat Bay offers only a tantalizing glimpse of heavily wooded McDonald Park campground, the seaside booktown of Sidney, with more bookstores per capita than anywhere else in Canada,

A junior men's four rowing team trains on Elk Lake.

Previous pages: Tsehum Harbour (All Bay) is located north of Sidney near the end of the Saanich Peninsula.

and the vegetable farms and federal Centre for Plant Health of North Saanich. It passes the bird-rich, fertile Martindale Flats of Central Saanich and climbs Cordwood Hill to suburban Tanner Ridge, then skirts Victoria's favourite swimming beaches at Elk Lake—where Canada's Olympic rowing team practises—and the sprawl of burbs and malls of Saanich (originally called South Saanich). As Blanshard Street it slows to a crawl through downtown Victoria and joins the Trans-Canada Highway (Highway 1) to end—though a diehard Victorian would claim this is where it all starts—at Mile 0 above the windy cliffs of Beacon Hill Park.

On the peninsula, crossroads punctuate the highway at intervals, and a few still retain their earliest settlement-era names, especially Mount Newton Cross Road, Stellys Cross Road, Keating Cross Road and Cedar Hill Cross Road. In the 19th century, when travel took much longer than it does today, these were the major routes across the peninsula and they still serve that purpose.

The peninsula's many neighbourhoods and districts make up four municipalities—counting the city of Saanich, which often gets lumped into "the core"—with a total area of 187 square kilometres (72.2 square miles). There were 152,285 residents in 2009, and the population of Saanich alone (113,516 in 2009) makes it the most populous municipality on Vancouver Island.

Many smaller West Coast fishboats are now disused or converted to pleasure craft.

On either side of the highway corridor, at varying distances, the 32-kilometre (20-mile) peninsula rolls away to the sea. At its widest in Saanich, where it joins the main body of Vancouver Island, the peninsula is upward of 15 kilometres (9.3 miles) across. At its narrowest point, just north of Victoria International Airport in North Saanich, it's about 2.5 kilometres (1.6 miles) across. Today its many kilometres of shoreline, ranging from sandy beaches to craggy cliffs, not only create abundant marine habitats for sea and shore life, they also attract visitors and residents with cameras or beach towels.

Even on sizzling summer weekends, the most accessible beaches are rarely crowded by eastern Canadian or European standards. Not every beach access promises a good picnic site or kayak launch, but should at least offer a striking viewpoint. Coles Bay faces west across busy Saanich Inlet toward Mill Bay, Lands End has a view north toward Cowichan Bay and Salt Spring Island, and Island View Beach faces east toward Haro Strait and its clusters of islands. The sea bounds the peninsula and naturally created some of its earliest and lasting industries.

The Saanich Peninsula shares the region's warm, sunny summers and mild winters, but is shielded from the worst of the stiff onshore winds that regularly blast Victoria and Esquimalt. Still, fall southwesters or wintry north winds can knock out electrical power for hours or even days in the peninsula's rural areas. The rugged hills and sheltered valleys create a hospitable environment of constantly changing seascapes and landscapes. On long summer evenings, when the copper sun melts below the dark Malahat Ridge across the inlet, even long-time residents will drift over to Deep Cove or Pat Bay to watch the sun go down.

A Place of Refuge

People have appreciated the beauty and fruitfulness of the peninsula for many years. Long ago Xals the Creator taught people to look after the land and its creatures, says a legend of the Wsanec (Saanich) people. When they grew careless, he sent a great flood to punish them. Some of the

Swan Lake Nature Sanctuary in Saanich is home to turtles, small mammals and many kinds of birds.

Harbour seals frequent offshore rocks around the Saanich Peninsula.

people made a long cedar rope and loaded their food and belongings into their canoes. As the waters rose higher, they paddled to the nearest mountain still above the water and tied up to a tall arbutus tree. Soon the water covered even the tallest trees on the mountain summit, and the people prayed to Xals to take pity. After many days a crow carrying a stick in its beak landed on the canoe and told the people the flood was receding. One of the men saw a distant mountain rising from the water and said, "Ni qennet tte wsanec," or "Look what is emerging." The Wsanec people landed on this mountain, which they called Lauwelnew (Place of Refuge), and gave thanks, and Xals promised never again to punish them with a flood. Wsanec people believe that Wolf and Thunderbird protected sacred sites high on the flanks of Lauwelnew, now called Mount Newton, and they are still used for ceremonial purposes.

Today four bands on the Saanich Peninsula trace their ancestry from these survivors: the Tsartlip, Pauquachin, Tseycum and Tsawout peoples. Together they founded Lauwelnew Tribal School on the peninsula to teach, among many other subjects, the story of their origin.

Wsanec villages once lined Brentwood Bay and Patricia Bay as well as the eastern shore of the peninsula from present-day Sidney south to Cordova Bay. In his book *Saltwater People*, Saanich elder Dave Elliott Sr. writes that the peninsula was the chief home of the Saanich people—even those from as far away as Washington state, the Comox area and the Sunshine Coast—who lived "from one end to the other and right around all the shore and all the bays" as well as on many of the Gulf Islands and all of the San Juans.

A trollerman who became a respected teacher and writer of Saanich history, Elliott also explains the place name: "Our word Wsanec in Saanich means 'raised up.' If you go offshore to the east and out into our territory and look west, you will see why. You'll see what it looks like in the distance compared to the surrounding land. It is 'raised up.'"

Elliott recalls that the Wsanec people used to travel throughout their territory as far south as Mount Douglas and Mount Finlayson to fish and gather food, making temporary housing wherever they stayed. He speaks of the endless wealth of their homeland: sea mammals and fish in the sea; shellfish, seaweed and seabird eggs on the shore; elk, deer and smaller creatures in the forest. His people also gathered cattails and grasses to weave into mats and baskets, and the fibres, leaves and berries of many plants for medicinal use. They dug and roasted camas bulbs in the oak meadows. The land provided generously, and supported an equally rich artistic and cultural life. Looking back at the time before the great smallpox epidemics and European settlement, many people see a golden age.

Lauwelnew Tribal School at Brentwood Bay teaches First Nations languages, history and culture.

Europeans saw something quite different. Even the affable Dr. J.S. Helmcken wrote of his 1850 arrival in Esquimalt, "These natives were… dirty greasy nasty-smelling creatures… very dark with black hair. Everyone had on a blanket… or in some cases less… we greenhorns could hardly distinguish the men from the women." (He later married and cherished James Douglas's partly Native and partly West Indian daughter Cecilia though.) However, farther north, early explorers such as Juan Francisco de la Bodega y Quadra valued and socialized with their aboriginal hosts.

As late as the 1850s, northerners—probably Comox and Kwakwaka'wakw raiders—attacked Wsanec villages, and groups living near Sidney moved over to Patricia Bay. Lekwungen people also had a village on the peninsula, before they moved closer to the new HBC fort on the Inner Harbour. Today the Saanich people live on four reserves on the peninsula. Against all odds they survived smallpox, the loss of traditional resources, the banning of the potlatch and decades of poverty, and elders now teach traditional language and culture not only to Saanich people but also to their non-aboriginal neighbours.

Into the Wilds

The deep wilderness of the Saanich Peninsula once daunted travellers who ventured to the rocky shores and deep forest, but they soon discovered what aboriginal people had known for millennia: that it is a rich and fertile area. The HBC originally designated the peninsula for the fur trade, and for convenience built a log storage barn in the area of present-day Reynolds School. After the Saanich treaties were signed in 1852, the HBC leased and later sold 40.47-hectare (100-acre) homesteads to farmers—and 80.94-hectare (200-acre) parcels to families—who cleared land for pasturage and field crops.

It was an immense undertaking to fell and burn sections of the towering first-growth forest for agriculture; farmers for generations would be burning stumps and picking stones out of their fields, thanks to the glacial deposits. Wildlife including cougars, bears, wolves, deer and elk ranged through their habitat. An umbrella, of all things, protected at least one early settler. Local history has it that a Saanich woman and her husband were homeward bound late one evening when a cougar threatened them; undeterred, the woman opened and closed her umbrella repeatedly to keep the cat at bay, allowing her husband time to run home for a rifle. The umbrella trick still features in "getting along with wildlife" brochures under tips for preventing cougar attacks.

Clusters of clearing and settlement sprang up near Craigflower Farm on the east bank of the Gorge Waterway, at Mount Tolmie, at Goldstream on Finlayson Arm and around Lauwelnew, which surveyor-general J.D. Pemberton had named Mount Newton after his draftsman. One of BC's oldest churches still in use today, St. Stephen's Anglican Church on Mount Newton Cross

Road, opened its doors in 1862 to serve the widely scattered population of the peninsula. Settlements at agricultural Gordon Head, at Saanichton and on the northern part of the peninsula followed over the next decades, and later grew up around seaside resort areas including Cadboro Bay and Cordova Bay.

Many families who settled the peninsula bought their land with their earnings from the goldfields on the Fraser River and later in the Cariboo. Miners passed through Victoria on their return from the goldfields to have their ore assayed; most quickly moved on, but those who stayed worked hard to transform wilderness into farmland. Others got their start in the up-island coal fields and later turned to farming. Their backgrounds were wonderfully varied: English, Scottish, Irish and Welsh, predictably, but also African-American, Asian and European. The settlers produced the basic necessities of life for the isolated colony—vegetables, tree fruits, grains, hay and livestock—and sold their goods in Victoria. In time they raised crops that gave less sustenance but more pleasure. The Vantreight family of Gordon Head succeeded famously with strawberries and daffodils. Another flower grower, Bill Mattick—his farm grew into today's thriving Mattick's Farm market and golf course—started the practice of shipping flowers every spring to winter-bound prairie towns, where they sold for shocking prices. Geoffrey Vantreight had wheedled daffodil bulbs from his neighbour William Edwards, whose daughter, Ursula Jupp, went on to write four delightful books on early Saanich and Victoria. The peninsula still grows huge numbers of fresh daffodils for commercial sale.

The Fruits of Their Labours

Other resource-based industries followed over the next century. Newcomers logged the great trees of the peninsula and skidded them down to tidewater at Brentwood and other bays. A few visionary pioneers including John Dean preserved untouched parcels of first-growth forest, which they bequeathed as parks. They fished the teeming inshore waters from Sidney, Brentwood Bay, Deep Cove and other small harbours, selling their catch to canneries in Victoria and Sidney. They dug gravel from glacial moraines and quarried limestone to make cement at Tod Inlet, on the site of today's Butchart Gardens. They also canned fruit in Sidney. Until the company moved to a less populated area up-island, they manufactured explosives at the Giant Powder Works on James Island.

Flower farms flourish on the Saanich Peninsula and the West Shore.

Commercial tulip fields cast a colourful blanket below Mount Newton.

Victoria families had picnicked, camped, fished, hunted and hiked on the peninsula from the earliest days, perhaps unconsciously imitating the First Peoples' annual travels through their territory to different harvest sites. Cottages, parks and camps sprang up on the Saanich shore of the Gorge and at spots including Cadboro Bay, Cordova Bay, Brentwood Bay, Deep Cove, Bazan Bay and Sidney. Friends and passersby appreciated a chance to visit the Butchart family's home Benvenuto (Italian for "welcome") and admire Jennie Butchart's wonderful gardens. She created garden after garden by having topsoil delivered by horse and cart from nearby Saanich farms, adding it to depleted limestone pits and planting familiar and exotic plants.

Farm carts, stagecoaches, transport drays and riding horses soon couldn't handle all the freight and passengers travelling between centres, so three railways were built in the 1890s to serve the peninsula and other parts of the region. Least successful, most irritating and yet most fondly remembered was the Victoria & Sidney Railway, nicknamed the "Cordwood Limited" because of its wood-burning steam locomotives' great appetite for wood. The train was also called the "tri-weekly," even though it ran daily, since it "tried weakly" and was infamous for rolling backward down its grades. After World War I, competition from motor vehicle traffic—despite roads that were axle-breaking deep in mud, boulders and roots—caused the decline of rail service, and it was discontinued in 1948. The V&S name survives in Central Saanich's Veyaness Road.

All three railways left a marvellous legacy in their rights-of-way, now part of the peninsula's vast network of walking, equestrian and biking trails. The Lochside and Galloping Goose trails together span the distance from Swartz Bay to downtown Victoria (the Galloping Goose goes all the way to Leechtown near Sooke); shorter trails pass through Colquitz River Park, the Rithet's Bog conservation area and Mount Douglas Park. The trail system also connects with an ever larger web of south-island trails and ultimately the Trans Canada Trail.

Water transportation in the early years was the easiest way for people to get from point to point on the peninsula and around wild Gordon Head, sunny Ten Mile Point and Oak Bay to

Above: Passengers on a BC Ferries vessel take advantage of the last sun.

Left: Orcas play in Juan de Fuca Strait; Mount Baker in Washington state is visible from the south island on most clear days.

Victoria. Square-rigged sailing ships brought most newcomers to the West Coast—a few "over-landers" made the long, arduous journey by land—but these ships made fewer local trips. Many early accounts describe travel by "Indian canoe" as newcomers hired aboriginal crews to carry passengers and freight swiftly and safely. A few newcomers bought small dugout canoes and mastered the art of balancing in the narrow, lightweight craft. Small sailboats, rowboats and later small gas-powered launches were also common, many of them made in south-island boatyards. Even today, old-time islanders assume that cadging a ride on a fishboat is a fine way to travel.

As the population grew, though, so did passenger and freight vessels. Canadian Pacific and Union steamships served the Inside Passage and as far north as Prince Rupert into the 1950s. Commercial aviation gradually replaced the up-coast steamers, and although some of the CP's Princess-class ships carried cars, there was growing demand for rapid car ferries to the Gulf Islands and the mainland. In 1960 the province created BC Ferries and started passenger and car runs from the small Swartz Bay terminal to a new terminal at Tsawwassen. The BC Ferries fleet now consists of fast vessels that make the Strait of Georgia crossing every two hours, and more often during the summer and holidays. Yet the ships are still folksy enough to stop to rescue a boater in trouble or to let passengers watch a passing orca pod.

In a class of its own is the tiny ferry that carries cars and passengers between Brentwood Bay and Mill Bay, a few kilometres south of Duncan. Now owned by BC Ferries, the *Mill Bay* has been on the job since 1958, replacing the earlier ferry *Brentwood* that made its first run in 1924. In those days the trip up-island via the steep, gravel Malahat Drive strained many cars to the limit, and dangerous washouts were common. Today the 25-minute ferry trip, running more or less hourly, is more of a pleasure than a necessity, except when construction or a bad accident affects "the Hat," now a well-maintained highway. BC Ferries advertises the Mill Bay route as "The Island's Most Beautiful Shortcut."

Local people cherish this ferry as a way to duck bumper-to-bumper recreational vehicles on the Hat and chat with fellow passengers, read a newspaper or catch a quick nap. It's less amusing if the captain takes a nap. In 1989, in one of the *Mill Bay*'s few accidents, the little ferry ran aground when the captain fell asleep; he hadn't slept after sailing the day before in Victoria's Swiftsure International Yacht Race.

On the Water and in the Air

Marine industry of all kinds has long played a part in the peninsula's life, and easy rail and motor travel from Victoria only increased its importance. Commercial marinas and government docks occupy every major bay, and private docks and jetties cling to the smallest coves and points all around the peninsula. Sailboats from sailing dinghies to square-rigged three-masters cruise these waters along with powerboats, canoes, kayaks and windsurfers. Canadian Navy ships routinely train and run exercises in Saanich Inlet and Haro Strait, and the Canadian Coast Guard docks next to the seaplane base at Patricia Bay. The Sidney North Saanich Yacht Club, snug in a heritage home on Tsehum Harbour (also called All Bay), runs regular courses, regattas and races.

All this marine traffic generates a demand for boat builders and services on the peninsula. Several boatyards specialize in wood hulls and especially classic wooden boats. Three marine supply stores in Sidney alone draw in people searching for the right cleat or just prowling through all the wonderful gear to dream about for next year's cruising. There are also rigging specialists, outboard and inboard engine services, propeller repair shops—not surprising in waters known for reefs and shoals—and sailmakers in Sidney and Brentwood Bay who can resew, patch or recut worn sails or build new sails made to measure. Since most of the sailmakers are sailors, one job perk is time off for regattas.

The Dominion Astrophysical Observatory began its study of the night sky in 1917 with a 1.8-metre (72-inch) telescope introduced by the first chief astronomer, John Plaskett. Briefly the largest in the world, the highly polished glass lens was transported through the Saanich wilderness and up rugged Observatory Hill trails by mule train, travelling along the edge of steep cliffs while astronomers held their collective breath. The DAO has logged many important discoveries since the telescope's first light, including groundbreaking work on methods for identifying exoplanets around distant stars and on charting near-earth objects such as asteroids or comets that could potentially strike our planet.

Opposite: MV *Mill Bay*, one of BC Ferries' smallest vessels, cruises past the Saanich Peninsula outward bound from its dock in Brentwood Bay.

The view from Dominion Astrophysical Observatory: overlooking the layered hills of Sooke; on clear evenings the observatory grounds offers an ideal vantage point for amateur astronomers.

Broader programs and a sophisticated computer system now dominate the observatory, which is now home to the Herzberg Institute of Astrophysics, but astronomers still use the venerable Plaskett telescope and two smaller telescopes almost every clear night. Amateur astronomers gather in the parking lot on clear Saturday evenings with their own equipment and welcome the public to come up and stargaze. The aptly named public interpretive site, the Centre of the Universe, features hands-on displays, lecture theatres, a small planetarium inside a septic tank—previously unused—and a shop crammed with heavenly gifts, books, computer programs and gadgets.

The flat fields just south and east of Sidney became a military aerodrome at the beginning of World War II. During the war it had a sizeable air force presence, which put nearby Sidney on the map as men and women in the service overflowed the small cannery and port town. Even into the 1950s people arriving by air were unnerved by the sight of apparent plane wrecks near the end of one runway; in fact it was just the spare parts heap.

Today Victoria International Airport's three runways buzz with air traffic including military flights and training, international and local commercial flights, aviation industry test flights, air rescue and air ambulance traffic, and several flight-training schools. A significant manufacturing industry is clustered on and around the airport. Viking Air alone employs about 400 people in manufacturing, repairing and converting de Havilland aircraft, including the historic Beaver, Otter and Twin Otter. The Twin Otter is the short takeoff and landing plane that—on wheels, skis and floats—opened up the remotest parts of the Canadian North to safe, dependable air traffic.

The history of flight in Canada and especially in the Victoria region is on view at the British Columbia Aviation Museum, located near the eastern limit of the airport, and those in search of more detail can satisfy both their curiosity and their hunger pangs at North Saanich's oldest café, Mary's Bleue Moon. Pictures of World War II air crews photographed there before flying overseas, model planes and parts of historic aircraft fill every available space on the walls and ceiling. Most days the café hums with the talk of commercial and private pilots, airport workers and air force crews from the 443 Maritime Helicopter Squadron. One sunny corner table facing the original airport terminal is said to be haunted by a spirit who enjoys their congenial company.

The British Columbia Aviation Museum near Sidney displays lovingly-restored early bush planes and war planes.

A Wealth of Gardens

Over many years, the Butcharts continued to develop spectacular new gardens in their former limestone quarry near Brentwood Bay. Jennie Butchart developed the large Sunken Garden first, then after a world tour followed it with the Japanese Garden. As the project expanded, the tennis court became the Italian Garden and the house's kitchen garden became the Rose Garden. By the 1920s the increasingly famous Butchart Gardens welcomed more than 50,000 visitors each year from all over the world. The factory stopped making cement in 1916 but made tiles and flower pots until 1950. All that remains of the original factory is a tall chimney that towers over the winding garden paths and fragrant borders as a reminder of the site's industrial origins. Still a family business, today the Butchart Gardens is Greater Victoria's number one tourist attraction, open year-round with many special events and offerings.

Opposite: A perennial favourite with visitors, the Butchart Gardens are especially lovely in springtime.

Local people mark two special occasions at the Butchart Gardens. One favourite is the garden at Christmas, usually decorated and specially lit from early December till early January, with scenes from the Twelve Days of Christmas cleverly placed in view of the walkways. A skating rink, carolling and live entertainment add to the experience. The second favourite is the Saturday-night closing fireworks display put on through the summer. To the delight of live-aboards and pleasure boaters at Brentwood Bay, these fireworks are also visible and audible from the dark waters there—without the cost of admission.

The displays are not quite so grand and polished at the Glendale Gardens & Woodland, tucked away in Saanich off West Saanich Road, but it is a working garden with many demonstration areas and green space—and admission costs roughly a third as much as it does at the Butchart Gardens. The emphasis here is on education. The Pacific Horticultural College is at Glendale, and courses and workshops for all ages are modestly priced throughout the year. The annual Glendale plant sales offer unusual shrubs and flowering plants—check the Glendale website for dates. It's a popular event, so you'll want to arrive early.

Walking paths through the University of Victoria's Finnerty Gardens offer an hour's quiet

Right: The Butchart Gardens' Christmas decorations and special events attract local people as well as tourists.

Below: Strawberry pickers' hands fly as they harvest Saanich Peninsula fields.

Bottom: Woodwynn Farm sweeps across the Mount Newton Valley in Central Saanich.

exercise or contemplation in any season without any admission charge, and on Sundays even the parking is free. Park near the university's Interfaith Chapel on the southwest side of the Fine Arts Building parking lot. The gardens are especially admired for their unusual rhododendrons, some of which grew from seeds gathered around the world by travelling botanists and gardeners.

The four peninsula municipalities—Saanich, Central Saanich, North Saanich and Sidney—and their key neighbourhoods still have a strong agricultural flavour. The 4-H Club thrives here for rural and suburban youths, and farm produce is the mainstay of farmers' markets held on different evenings in different communities through the summer. The Saanich Fair, held every Labour Day weekend, draws an average of 45,000 people to enjoy the exhibits and entertainment. Organized by the non-profit North and South Saanich Agricultural Society, the fair depends on hundreds of volunteers to run the event at the 28.3-hectare (70-acre) fairground on Stellys Cross Road in Central Saanich. As well as livestock events, live entertainment, a midway, craft and skills exhibitions, and a farmers' market, the fair offers a fine arts show, a photography show and historical displays. The Saanich Fair was first held in 1868 and is one of Canada's largest and longest-running agricultural fairs.

Places to Be, Places to See

Today residential neighbourhoods and compact shopping areas predominate in the peninsula, including some much-admired specialty shops and boutiques in Sidney and Cordova Bay, making the old agricultural and marine industrial base less visible. A new commercial-residential complex in Saanich called Uptown is intended to create a core for the increasingly urban community on Victoria's northern boundary. The dreary rows of boxy houses that afflict some cities certainly make an appearance throughout the area, but for the most part, the peninsula municipalities have rejected high-density residential developments and big-box retailers. Instead they've embraced farmers' markets, farm-gate sales and arts tours. Parks, green spaces, hiking and biking paths, and public-access beaches are numerous.

The municipality of Saanich is essentially urban in its southern reaches, where it borders Victoria, and many attractions that people consider part of Victoria actually lie within Saanich's boundaries. Several of the region's biggest shopping malls are here: Tillicum, upscale Broadmead and Victoria's first mall, Town and Country, now transformed into the Uptown complex. Half of the University of Victoria campus and both campuses of Camosun College fall within Saanich, along with several technology parks. Cyclists and hikers appreciate the views from Mount Tolmie Park and Mount Douglas Park, and paddlers and picnickers choose the beaches at Cadboro Bay's Gyro Park, Agate Beach in Cordova Bay and Arbutus Cove. Saanich industries range from Latitude Technologies, which produces airborne tracking systems, to Babe's Honey, which processes wax and honey and offers retail sales from its unmistakable honey-gold building visible from Oldfield Road.

The lush Central Saanich fields that you see from the Pat Bay Highway and up on the central plateau produce a mixed basket of vegetables, fruits, livestock, grains and forage. Visitors and city folks encounter country life when they shop at Central Saanich farm gates or farmers' markets and when they attend the Saanich Fair; among its heady scents of freshly cut grass and fresh baking,

Some visitors are more colourful than others: monarch butterflies migrate through BC every year and sometimes breed on the south island.

The University of Victoria's Finnerty Gardens are noted for their unusual rhododendrons, many of them collected by far-travelling botanists.

Iconic and photogenic, the Fish Market sits on Sidney Pier at the foot of Beacon Avenue.

the fair displays rural life at its best. Subdivisions are few and scattered in Central Saanich, and the closest thing to density housing is a few well-designed condo complexes near the shopping centre of Saanichton. Yet around Keating Cross Road, where fruit packers and agricultural equipment dealers once dominated, small manufacturers and industries now pack new buildings in a small industrial zone. Farther east on Tod Inlet and Saanich Inlet lie the magical worlds of the Butchart Gardens and Victoria Butterfly Gardens, the latter being a fine place to relax on a rainy winter afternoon while delicate, brilliant flying creatures land on your shoulders. The Saanich Historical Artifacts Society just north of Island View Road provides a fascinating glimpse of pioneer history; you can round out your visit with a walk along the beach or pathways at Island View Beach Park. Just north on beautiful Brentwood Bay are marine industries, marinas and the Brentwood–Mill Bay ferry, overlooked by the dockside Seahorses Café.

North Saanich retains a strongly rural atmosphere of farms, plant nurseries, vineyards, country B&Bs and small rural industries, yet it also contains the Victoria International Airport and the BC Ferries terminal (the Washington State Ferries terminal is in nearby Sidney), a handful of large and small marinas, several subdivisions, two major federal research institutions and aviation-related companies. At the northern end of the peninsula, North Saanich's heritage Garry oaks and broad farm fields occupy relatively level ground closer to sea level than other parts of the region—the airport elevation is only 19.2 metres (63 feet)—though several hills

Every year 1.5 million travellers pass through Victoria International Airport.

provide good walking in relatively undeveloped parks. As the crow flies, the peninsula is only about 2.5 kilometres (1.6 miles) across at its narrowest point, yet you can count on the weather at Deep Cove, the airport and Lands End being different. Two fly-in cafés serve the airport and its high-tech industries: the Dakota Café at the Victoria Flying Club and the Spitfire Grill at the western side of the airport near the air force base.

The seashore town of Sidney, looking east from within the boundaries of North Saanich, is a compact shopping and residential centre with a sunny character all its own. It's taken to calling

Above left: Shooting stars and other wildflowers line the wilderness trails of John Dean Park in North Saanich.

Above: A rare snowfall decorates boats at Canoe Cove Marina near Sidney. The effect is pretty but damaging; after a heavy snowfall unattended craft can sink under the extra weight.

itself "Sidney by the Sea" and "Sidney Booktown," the latter thanks to former MLA and MP Clive Tanner and his wife, Christine, who have owned several bookstores and encouraged the development of others. About a dozen bookstores—new, used, bargain, collector, mystery, paperback, specialty—line the streets. Sidney's piers, waterfront parks and careful development over the past two decades mean it's no longer a sleepy one-storey town that needed only a grain elevator to fit anywhere in the prairies. People with limited mobility appreciate Sidney's level streets and general accessibility, giving rise to jokes about scooter gangs—two scooters abreast on a Sidney sidewalk means pedestrians walk in the street—and younger people in search of a dance, concert or club are likely to head for downtown Victoria. Several new upscale hotels and a good selection of ethnic restaurants and fine dining draw off-island and regional visitors, who also shop Sidney's eclectic offering of boutiques, art galleries and gift shops. The Shaw Ocean Discovery Centre and Sidney Museum are other attractions, and the small, two-screen Star Theatre is one of the town's treasures.

Real estate listings throughout the peninsula turn up everything from modest condos and tiny cottages to splendidly landscaped waterfront estates with houses better described as mansions; North Saanich ranks second only to Oak Bay in housing prices and incomes, and the other municipalities aren't far behind. Planned communities such as Dean Park and Broadmead and gated condo complexes are not common, however; there's still enough of hard-working, down-to-earth Saanich to smile at these manicured enclaves.

The people who work and play on the peninsula today still inhabit a rolling landscape of daffodil farms, vineyards and orchards bounded by stretches of beaches and seashore, and are served by small towns and crossroad stores more than by malls. Yet rural lifestyle is no longer the norm; high school classes no longer lose half their students to hay harvesting, daffodil picking or strawberry picking as they did only a few decades ago. Some things change, some things remain. On a foggy winter day, when the ravens wheel creaking over the dark wooded heights, Lauwelnew, the place of refuge, still watches over a landscape scoured clean and rebuilt by glaciers and shifting sea levels more than humans will ever change it.

West Shore: Gearing Up for Growth

West of Victoria and its long-settled core

municipalities lies a region of dizzying diversity that includes timeless seashores on the open Pacific Ocean, old farmland, wilderness parks, suburban subdivisions and a shopper's paradise of high-energy, newly uncrated mall sprawl.

Right: Sheep also seem to admire a blooming daffodil field.

Previous pages: Pease Lake is one of several lakes tucked away in Highlands.

Times change, but rarely do they change more dramatically than in the once sleepy western communities of southern Vancouver Island. Generations ago, small-time gold miners arrived on horseback to chip away at bedrock or pan gold in placer operations where tidy provincial parks now welcome

The grass is greener in rural Metchosin.

visitors in RVs. A country gas station once sold bait for fishing on the Millstream where big-box stores now sell almost anything imaginable to anyone with money in hand and a vehicle to carry off the loot.

By Victoria standards, the West Shore lives on a larger and sometimes more boisterous scale. Its rural pockets are a fine refuge for people who don't fit neatly among Victoria's manicured lawns and gardens; its town centres and commercial districts draw shoppers from all over the mid-island, Gulf Islands and south island.

Many people are new arrivals from points east—at times the whole place seems to have been airlifted straight from the outskirts of Calgary—either because they recoiled in shock from higher housing prices in Victoria, Oak Bay and Saanich or because of the area's boundless vitality.

Steep hillsides, craggy outcrops of dark volcanic bedrock and dramatic shorelines lashed by storms characterize the West Shore's natural landscape, but there are also peaceful valley farms, Garry oak meadows and some of the region's finest recreational parks and beaches. The south island's complex geological past of colliding terranes, or sections, of the earth's crust means that ancient rocks are visible, and not always in the obvious places. Look for strongly tilted beds of ribbon chert, slate and schist of the Leech River Formation around Goldstream Provincial Park in Langford.

Wild animals once roamed freely in the western communities, but now human residents share their territory, usually peaceably. Occasionally a cougar kills a sheep or a dog on a Metchosin farm, and angry householders chase off raccoons that knock over garbage cans. Much more often the parks, beaches and walking trails attract recreational hikers and bikers, children's outdoor education classes and dedicated birdwatchers.

A young aboriginal fisherman nets a salmon in Goldstream Provincial Park.

In the past industry, not recreation, drew most people to the West Shore area. Long ago it was the rich food sources of the beaches, streams, offshore waters and adjacent lands that led aboriginal groups to make seasonal and year-round settlements. As in other parts of the south island, the forests, meadows and lakes provided the materials for cedar houses and canoes, stone or copper tools, bark clothing, grass and reed baskets, and seasonal foods including ducks, berries and camas bulbs.

First Peoples have lived in the western communities for at least 3,000 years at various locations, according to a fascinating guidebook to the region's archeology, *Victoria Underfoot*. Recent archeological digs have examined some of these sites, finding beautifully made ancient tools, weapons and baskets. Archeologists have identified village sites, middens and burial places at Fort Rodd Hill and a settlement at Esquimalt Lagoon, both in Colwood.

Spanish naval explorers charted the West Shore as early as the late 1770s; the first European who recorded his landing in this region was Manuel Quimper in 1790, aboard the *Princesa Real*. It is possible, though, that English explorer and privateer Francis Drake sailed past in the summer of 1579 in the *Golden Hinde* during his circumnavigation of the world.

European settlers first came to the western communities for the Hudson's Bay Company, and stayed to farm, fish, mine and log the area's rich resources and provide services to others who followed. Local museums showcase the early history with displays and artwork, and a wealth of documentary information lies in their archives.

This Way Forward

The West Shore has a past, and an interesting past at that, but more to the point it has a future. The five communities lying to the west and northwest of Victoria will experience the area's greatest growth and expansion, partly through geographical necessity—there's really nowhere else to grow; the population is forecast to double over the next 20 years, with the fastest growth in Colwood and Langford—and partly because of the residents. This is an area where young families predominate

Following pages: Emerging from a sea of fog, hills on the Saanich Peninsula look like islands from a viewpoint on the Malahat Drive.

and the municipalities, after some rocky starts, have shown considerable flair and innovation in rethinking and developing an area where sprawl had taken its natural course for a century.

View Royal, Colwood, Langford, Highlands and Metchosin—the West Shore municipalities—are largely off the beaten track for casual visitors. They're not in the standard tourist guides, for the most part. They're even a little out of the way for those living in Victoria's core. That's their loss. The vast West Shore area contains not only up-and-coming commercial districts but an eclectic mix of attractions, including Langford's race-car shrine Western Speedway—Canada's oldest auto-racing track—with its paved oval track and seating for 4,000. There are also spectacular Goldstream Provincial Park, the one-of-a-kind Cloth Castle for quilters and sewers and Colwood's historic Hatley Castle, an astonishing extravaganza of West Coast Edwardian architecture that is now part of Royal Roads University.

Wide-open beaches, gorgeous parks and pristine wilderness are also part of the mix on the West Shore, which stretches around southern Vancouver Island from Esquimalt Harbour west to Rocky Point, the island's southernmost point of land.

There are other attractions, of course. If eateries say a certain amount about their locale, the western communities' restaurants say a lot. Elegant dining is certainly available at establishments such as Evedar's Bistro, but the cafés and pubs with lineups at the door and parking lots overflowing with pickup trucks say a whole mouthful. Favourites include Four Mile House in View Royal, Smoken Bones Cookshack in Langford, My-Chosen Cafe in Metchosin and the Chequered Flag Café on the road to the racetrack. The helpings are generous, the servers are friendly even when they're rushed off their feet and the rooms hum with conversation.

View Royal: The Portage

At the heart of View Royal lies a traditional portage route used for millennia by First Peoples and by early settlers in the days when travel was easier by water than by land. The portage, of only a few

West Shore communities are the fastest-growing on the south island.

hundred metres, led from Esquimalt Harbour on Juan de Fuca Strait across the Esquimalt Peninsula to the protected Gorge Waterway and Victoria Harbour. Even today, View Royal is a transportation nexus where the Old Island Highway secondary route to the West Shore and Sooke crosses the Trans-Canada Highway heading up-island, effectively quartering the municipality. In 1983 this major intersection was deemed the ideal place to build the new Victoria General Hospital.

View Royal lives up to its name with panoramas across hills, valleys and waters. Only 14.5 square kilometres (5.6 square miles) in area, and having only 9,583 residents in 2009, View Royal dazzles with some of the region's favourite swimming holes, boating spots and parks.

Portage Park on Esquimalt Harbour preserves the site of the old canoe portage from Portage Inlet to the head of Esquimalt Harbour. It makes for a cool walk through leafy, mostly deciduous, woodland over part of the old portage trail, now surrounded by subdivisions. Many shade wildflowers and native plants grow in the park, an important habitat for rare species. A First Nations midden discovered there has been radiocarbon-dated as 2,800 years old, and archeologists have also found layered animal remains and signs of settlement.

"The old portage trail is in the dip under the railway bridge below Four Mile House," View Royal resident William Stavdal explains, and he can point out the crease in the underbrush visible from the Old Island Highway. The portage saved hours of cross-country slogging for First Peoples, early settlers and at least one notable visitor in 1861, he says: "Lady Franklin was paddled up here when she was raising support to search for the lost Franklin expedition."

Thetis Lake Regional Park includes 833.7 hectares (2,060 acres) of marshes, meadows and Douglas fir and Garry oak habitats. It also offers kilometres of trails and several linked lakes for canoeing and freshwater swimming—the region's best, many would say—in a peaceful wilderness setting. View Royal Park includes 1.5 kilometres (about a mile) of easy walking trails near Craigflower Creek. The Upper Gorge Waterway and most of Portage Inlet, in places only a stone's throw from the Trans-Canada Highway, are a kayaker's and birdwatcher's paradise.

Wildflowers including false lily of the valley flourish in hidden glades every spring and summer.

Lily pads crowd a cove at Thetis Lake in View Royal.

Craigflower Manor has looked out toward the Gorge Waterway for more than a century and a half.

John Helmcken, the HBC doctor at Fort Victoria, recognized the area's beauty and bought a section of land (259 hectares, or 640 acres) from his employers in the 1850s. In 1853, Craigflower Farm, one of the four original farms created by the HBC-subsidiary Puget Sound Agricultural Company, broke ground nearby for farming on the Upper Gorge. Craigflower operated in the way the HBC understood, as a European estate with hired labourers expected to obediently do any menial task. Unsurprisingly, there were protests over working conditions. Only weeks after their arrival in 1853, some employees were refusing to work.

Craigflower never lived up to expectations for selling farm produce as far north as Russian Alaska and as far south as Oregon Territory, but it became the hub of a more successful private farming community. The Georgian-style wooden Craigflower Farmhouse is now a national historic site. Craigflower School, built nearby in 1855, is the oldest surviving schoolhouse in western Canada. Both are maintained by The Land Conservancy and open to visitors during the summer months. A tour of the two-storey manor's rooms gives a strong flavour of the early Victorian West Coast, and it's a favourite among school groups and historical re-enactors.

After flooding damaged his sawmill, driven by a water wheel on the Millstream at the head of Esquimalt Harbour, manager William Parson bought 40 acres (about 17 hectares) of what is now View Royal from the HBC in 1855 and opened a hotel near the Millstream bridge. At first Parson's Bridge Hotel catered to Royal Navy officers; later, called Six Mile House, it survived fires, floods and prohibition. Today it is one of BC's oldest pubs. A few kilometres east on the old Island Highway,

Four Mile House evolved from another 1850s cottage. There, owner Peter Calvert served refreshments to stagecoach travellers en route to Colwood, Langford or Sooke. Much later, after a few years in the late 1940s as a notorious roadhouse brothel called the Lantern House Inn, the building was abandoned. The present owners renovated it and now operate Four Mile House as a sports bar and a restaurant known for meals and afternoon teas in a heritage setting—and for its historic ghosts.

For nearly a century people have been seeing The White Lady standing on the rocks near the pub, looking out to sea; Peter Calvert's grandson Wilf Gouge identified her as his great-aunt, who lived with his family early in the 20th century while she waited for her sea captain husband to come home. Every day she would walk to nearby Thetis Point and scan the sea for ships, and when she died before her husband's return, she was buried there.

A woman in a long gown has also been seen standing at an upstairs window looking out at the gardens, and a man in an old-fashioned suit has been seen sitting at a dining room table. Some of the ghosts clearly have a sense of humour and like to play tricks on the kitchen staff, hiding small objects until asked for their return.

View Royal grew up around these early establishments and developed into today's rather scattered, easygoing district. Its residential areas vary from humble cottages built one room at a time over the last hundred years to waterfront mansions looking out across Portage Inlet and Esquimalt Harbour toward ocean sunsets. Its commercial elements range from corner stores and funky pizzerias to the huge View Royal Casino that presides over a strip development of car dealerships along the Island Highway. It's a challenge to capture the character of View Royal, but while you're contemplating it, you can try your luck at blackjack or paddle a canoe in a wilderness lake system.

Colwood: A Defensible Position

A hotheaded gentleman farmer's nostalgia for the old country gave Colwood its name. Captain Edward Langford, who would be the manager of the HBC-subsidiary Esquimalt Farm (also known as Colwood Farm and Mill Farm) from 1851 to 1861, enlivened Victoria's social scene by bringing his wife and five pretty daughters to the settlement of a few hundred Europeans, mostly men. Their new home was described by the HBC as a house with a garden, a flock of sheep (tended by Kanakas or Hawaiians, many of whom who came to the island with the HBC), servants' cottages, waterfrontage and a pier.

High Victorian style made for a gracious life at Craigflower Manor.

Their stay was stormy from the first day, when they discovered the HBC had provided not a pleasant house but two one-room huts. A kindly minister and his wife took the family in, and soon afterward Mrs. Langford gave birth to the area's first non-aboriginal male child. Once they were able to move in, the family named their new home Colwood after their former farm in Sussex, England. For 10 years Captain Langford entertained lavishly and quarrelled with James Douglas over HBC policy, claiming that he'd been treated unjustly, then packed up and returned in high dudgeon to England. Ironically, this family—who lived here so briefly and discontentedly—left behind names for the lively municipalities of Langford and western Canada's southernmost city, Colwood.

Other early Scottish and English immigrants had happier experiences and stayed to farm, plant orchards and raise livestock, though the HBC never drew as many settlers to the south island as hoped, partly because land was free to homesteaders elsewhere in British North America but relatively expensive at one pound per acre for settlers on HBC-managed Vancouver Island. It took the discovery of gold on the Fraser River in 1858 to spark any significant growth. Other small West

Shore businesses that sprang up to support the community included logging companies, sawmills, stone and gravel quarries, hotels, a tannery and a shoe factory.

Colwood, despite its small size—17.8 square kilometres (6.9 square miles) with 16,174 residents in 2009—contains several of the region's best-loved recreational spots. The three favourites lay on some of the region's most striking seascapes, where photographers and artists work to capture the shoreline, marine traffic and distant mountains.

Fisgard Lighthouse is older than Canada, dating from the time when Vancouver Island was still a Crown colony. Built in 1860 on small Fisgard Island at the entrance to Esquimalt Harbour, BC's first permanent lighthouse is still operational after a century and a half, though an automated system replaced the lighthouse keeper in 1929. A causeway was later built to permanently connect the lighthouse to the shore. The rounded bricks used in constructing the lighthouse, carefully carved to shape and numbered for reassembly, came around Cape Horn from England by sailing ship. The great lighthouse lantern originally burned coal oil and later gas, but today depends on electricity.

Visitors enjoy touring the 19th-century lighthouse tower and the adjacent two-storey red brick lightkeeper's house, which contain historical exhibits on the hard life of an early lighthouse keeper, complete with shipwrecks, storms and grinding isolation. Access to the lighthouse is through the national historic site of Fort Rodd Hill.

A Russian invasion that never arrived in the late 19th century sparked the construction of Fort Rodd, overlooking Esquimalt Harbour and its western approaches. In its heyday the coastal defence fort had three gun batteries, underground magazines for ammunition, barracks, guardhouses, command posts and powerful searchlights. The last British troops left the fort in 1906, and in 1956 its Canadian artillery units stood down, unneeded in an age of air defence. The old fort stood empty for several years, falling into disrepair, but it was declared a national historic site in 1958. Over the last four decades Parks Canada has stabilized and restored the site based on Royal Engineers records from 1903–5. Today the beautiful seashore and parkland of Fort Rodd Hill, as well as most of the original buildings, commemorate the early coastal defence of Victoria and Esquimalt. Exhibits, historical re-enactments and picnic sites with world-class views make the old fort a popular destination for visitors and residents.

The fine beach and gently sloping oak meadows of Colwood are part of the traditional territory of the Lekwungen (Songhees) people and for many centuries supported aboriginal settlements. Some highly developed tools and weapons have come to light in archeological digs at more than 45 sites. After James Douglas signed treaties with the Songhees people, he purchased about 100 hectares (247 acres) at Rodd Hill and founded Belmont Farm, later the home of his brother-in-law David Cameron. Other settlers gradually moved to the area, making Colwood a busy rural community by the early 20th century.

Hatley Castle was built in 1908 in full-on Edwardian style by James Dunsmuir, the son of coal entrepreneur Robert Dunsmuir, who had built his own Craigdarroch Castle in Victoria. A reluctant BC premier and later lieutenant-governor, James Dunsmuir spared no expense to build his waterfront residence with a fortune garnered from the world's most dangerous mines up-island at Nanaimo and Cumberland. The turreted mansion has spectacular gardens and grounds—once maintained by a hundred employees—and occupies a former Northern Straits Salish burial site overlooking Esquimalt Lagoon. James Dunsmuir occupied his fine home through family feuds, an unhappy political career and the death of his favourite son, James "Boy" Dunsmuir, in the 1915 sinking of the *Lusitania*. In 1940 the federal government bought the property and operated it as a military college, Royal Roads, until 1995, when it was closed to make way for Royal Roads University.

Today Royal Roads maintains the century-old castle and its gardens, popular with visitors and

Opposite: Fisgard Lighthouse and adjacent Fort Rodd Hill are now a national historic site.

wedding parties. The university will soon also house the Robert Bateman Centre for art and environmental studies, honouring the well-known wildlife artist, in a building that will generate its own solar power and make sustainable use of water in harmony with its wetland setting.

Not far from Royal Roads is one of the region's finest spots for birdwatching, Esquimalt Lagoon. Numerous resident shorebirds, waterfowl and woodland species thrive here among the gravel bars and islets, but many migrants also make an appearance. The lovely setting between land and sea tempts photographers to wait patiently for the perfect shot.

Colwood is pursuing a green approach to other new developments and civic projects, including electric city vehicles, support for local food and agriculture, an energetic tree-planting program in city parks and ecologically friendly transportation, street lighting and wastewater treatment. Although Colwood hasn't seen the population explosion and burgeoning financial success of its bigger neighbour Langford, it is enjoying steady growth along sustainable lines. New residents and businesses are increasingly drawn by the expanding university, new housing developments with spectacular sea views and the city's can-do attitude.

BC Premier and entrepreneur James Dunsmuir built Hatley Castle, now the home of Royal Roads University. If it looks surprisingly familiar, you may have seen it as a movie set.

Langford: City on Wheels

Langford may not yet have achieved the village atmosphere of Oak Bay Avenue or Sidney's Beacon Avenue, but give it a couple of years.

Boutiques, city offices, library and coffee shops line Langford's "downtown" on Goldstream Avenue between Jacklin Road and Millstream Road, where locals with laptops take advantage of the free wireless internet. People bicycle and walk the city's extensive trail system—several lakes lie within easy reach and the Galloping Goose Trail swings inside city boundaries—though chrome-laden pickup trucks might still outnumber them on major roads. Skaters glide on an outdoor rink through the winter months, and families ride the free-or-donation Langford Trolley from outlying residential districts and around a circuit of mall shops and downtown businesses.

A decade ago Langford dreamed of becoming a new high-tech centre to revitalize the scattered community and attract new businesses. Everyone was on-side except the high-tech companies, as it turned out. An effort to boost tourism didn't pan out either. What next? How to inject new life—money, in other words—into a largely rural municipality of run-down neighbourhoods and weary strip malls?

Other south island communities had mostly turned up their noses at giant chain stores like Costco, Walmart, Home Depot and Canadian Tire. Langford took a collective deep breath and opened its doors to business. Today it's one of the fastest-growing municipalities in the region, with 27,328 residents in 2009 living within its 39.5 square kilometres (15.3 square miles).

Incomes, ages and housing prices are all still lower on the average than in the core municipalities to the south and east, but cash flows through the big-box stores and factory outlets. Victoria residents happily drive out to Langford for discount office equipment, bulk foods and cheaper gasoline. The money flows in, and the result is visible in sustainable civic projects.

Trees are everywhere in Langford despite its asphalt-and-concrete expanse of malls, highways and overpasses. Even fading malls and residential neighbourhoods, left behind by the glossy new

A clown and bull rider give their best to a local rodeo.

megamalls and burbs, are set within a leafy green landscape. And as in most of the Victoria region, any spare corner of public land is planted to within an inch of its life with flourishing shrubbery and colourful flowers.

All of this might bemuse those who once sneered at Langford as the region's crass, gritty "dogpatch." These days no one who's paying attention utters the d-word. It's not just that long-time mayor Stew Young might well challenge the speaker to a duel, it's also the area's strong, even defiant, sense of community and considerable vision in planning and development. The place now crackles with energy, excitement, money and ideas.

Among the area's favourite events are the Luxton Spring Rodeo and the Luxton Fall Fair, both held at the fairgrounds near Glen Lake on the southwestern side of the municipality. This is still horse country, with perhaps less emphasis on equitation than on exciting rough-and-tumble performances. Local and visiting riders compete in the rodeo each year, and the fall fair features exhibits of livestock, agricultural and garden produce, demonstrations of antique farm equipment and blacksmithing, crafts and a midway.

A family outing on the Galloping Goose Trail can occupy an hour or a weekend.

In all the best ways, old-time Langford is still there under the high gloss. Every south-island schoolchild has spent a late autumn afternoon at Goldstream watching the chum salmon fight their way upstream to spawn. If manicured Beacon Hill Park defines and embraces Victoria South, the northern bracket is the wilderness of Goldstream Provincial Park.

The park straddles the head of Finlayson Arm, a traditional aboriginal fishing ground where the Goldstream River reaches tidewater in a salt marsh set aside as a quiet zone for bird and wildlife watching. Shady vales and huge mossy old-growth rainforest cedars and firs dominate the park,

Chum salmon spawn and die on the Goldstream every year, playing their last part in the cycle of death and renewal.

but its 388 hectares (about 960 acres) also include sunny ridges where arbutus, lodgepole pine and dogwood trees flourish.

A handful of trails, from easy strolling to mountainous, lead to the spectacular falls on Niagara Creek, to the top of Mount Finlayson (419 metres, about 1,375 feet) and along the Goldstream River, where they are known as the Prospectors' or Gold Mine trails. Lieutenant Peter Leech of the Royal Engineers discovered traces of gold here in 1858; he later touched off a gold rush on the Leech River near Sooke. Miners dug holes and shafts that are still visible near the Goldstream, but little gold repaid their efforts.

An interpretive centre, a campground and a picnic area draw a steady trickle of local visitors throughout the year and a flood in the summer months. Even in torrential rain Goldstream is an impressive spot, and in filtered sunshine its beauty is magical.

Other municipal and regional parks offer walking and cycling paths and picnic areas, and help to preserve the best of Langford's rural origins.

No description of Langford would be complete without mentioning the sometimes controversial Bear Mountain golf resort—it boasts 36 holes on mountain and valley courses designed by Jack Nicklaus—and its accompanying residential neighbourhood. Whatever local people think of the development itself, the complex created as many as a thousand jobs in the municipality, and according to Mayor Young, made it possible, along with the big-box stores, to lower property taxes slightly instead of raising them.

Langford has earned awards for its careful planning and its new emphasis on a sustainable, liveable environment for all ages, but this is also a cautionary tale: the municipality, which first sprang up around farms and country stores, grew higgledy-piggledy for a century and needed

considerable replanning. Fortunately it's been a great success, except perhaps for the society-shy eccentrics and deeply rural folk who've edged farther out from the city lights—a reminder that while the south island has many charms, it has a dwindling number of truly remote areas.

Top left: Pease Lake in Highlands.

Above: A springtime array of fawn lilies brightens St. Mary the Virgin Anglican Church in Metchosin.

Highlands: Far From the Sprawl

Not a single shopping mall graces the West Shore municipality of Highlands, where many small home-based businesses serve their clientele without fanfare; some weeks the most exciting local event is the volunteer firefighters' practice evening. That's the way people like it here—quiet— though community spirit drives its craft fairs and Christmas hampers, drop-in coffee house and Volunteer of the Month program. The almost exclusively residential Highlands district occupies the opposite end of the spectrum from Langford, and may have attracted some of those fleeing the sprawl and malls. Its 37.9 square kilometres (14.6 square miles) make it just slightly smaller than Langford, but with 2,175 residents in 2009 it had only a tenth of Langford's population.

Highlands lies north of Langford and View Royal at the southwest end of the Saanich Peninsula, and commands some of the region's most glorious upland scenery as well as some of its most challenging wilderness parks. Gowlland Tod Provincial Park, Mount Work Regional Park and Francis/King Regional Park—where naturalists say the forest is 10,000 years old—all have hiking and biking trails, some of which follow old logging and mining roads, that range in difficulty from granny-and-toddler level to tough grinds. The district is as steep as its name suggests; much of it looks west over Finlayson Arm or, from the Willis Point neighbourhood, north down Saanich Inlet to the southern Gulf Islands.

Apart from adventurous souls heading for the wilderness parks, Highlands is more of a draw

for its residents than for visitors, unless they're eyeing the multi-million-dollar waterfront properties that occasionally turn up on the market. By south island standards, Highlands is not prime commuter territory—it can take most of an hour to get to some parts to downtown Victoria, occasionally longer when there's snow at higher elevations—but that has never deterred those hardy Highlanders who make the drive daily.

Years ago the Highlands was tarred with a reputation for hillbillies and crime, mostly undeserved. Now it's a beautiful retreat of the wealthy and the independent-minded who cherish their largely unspoiled natural environment. There will be no big-box stores opening here in the foreseeable future. Highlands is a world unto itself, a world of its own making.

Metchosin: A Scent of Apples

A municipality with a name that translates as "place of stinking fish" isn't necessarily where you'd expect to find natural beauty, intensive agriculture and artistic talent by the wheelbarrow-load, but Metchosin excels at contrasts and surprises.

Metchosin stretches along the island's sunny southeast-facing shore, south of Langford between Colwood to the east and Sooke to the west. Its 71.3 square kilometres (27.5 square miles) make it the largest West Shore municipality, almost twice the size of next-largest Langford, but its 2009 population was a thinly scattered 5,133. Relatively level compared to its inland neighbours, Metchosin's landscape includes long beaches scoured by Juan de Fuca Strait waters, rolling Garry oak meadows, woodland studded with sunny arbutus-crowned outcrops, and long-settled farmsteads with old wood-frame houses and orchards of fruit trees bearing varieties from another century.

Metchosin's beaches, wetlands and fire-controlled meadows richly supported a First Nations population for millennia before the first European turned up near Albert Head. Lieutenant Manuel Quimper of the prize ship *Princesa Real* carved a cross on a tree, buried a glass bottle among its roots, claimed the area for Spain and departed forever. Stories later claimed that local Northern Straits Salish people immediately dug up the bottle, but two centuries later people were still searching in vain for the carved tree. Settlers first moved in to farm the area not long after the HBC founded Fort Victoria at Camosun. Metchosin's Pioneer Museum and School Museum both provide a wealth of information about the municipality's early years.

The natural beauty and open landscape of the area appeal strongly to the eye, so why didn't Metchosin become the site of the new HBC fort and ultimately the capital of a colony and province? James Douglas admired Metchosin as a "very pretty place" with fresh water, but wrote, "There is, however, no Harbor, and the Anchorage is exposed, and must be insecure in Rough Weather." He also felt that the rolling, stony ground would not produce enough food for the fort.

Metchosin has a sense of community to match its beauty; gentleman farmers who prefer not to mention their family titles, retirees from eastern climes, loggers and mechanics may rub elbows in the coffee shop or at council meeting. A lively online forum sees discussion of international aid fundraising, litter, cougar sightings, found cats and other local interests ("wanted: milking machine").

Writer Tom Henry captured this flavour in his CBC Radio spots, collated into his 1996 book *Dogless in Metchosin*: the combination of resilience, curiosity, hard work and goofiness that a newcomer needs to thrive here.

The closest thing Metchosin has to a downtown is the commercial cluster near the corner of Metchosin Road and Happy Valley Road. Businesses that thrive in the area range from natural foods producers to day spas to B&Bs, plus the requisite woodworkers, dog trainers, general store, auto repair, cafés, artists, landscapers and excavators. It's debatable whether Metchosin is the most

Opposite: Sitting Lady Falls on Bilston Creek rewards visitors to Witty's Lagoon Regional Park in Metchosin.

Above: A sentry post at minimum-security William Head Institution in Metchosin overlooks not only the prison but Race Rocks and the Olympic Peninsula in Washington state.

Right: Lester B. Pearson United World College in Metchosin offers full scholarships for international students of exceptional promise and potential.

Poppies make a splash of wild colour among the green fields and woodlands of the rural south island.

rural part of the Victoria region—the Highlands and parts of the Saanich Peninsula might challenge that—but its intense sense of community makes it feel sociable, if not idyllic. Tom Henry claimed that his life in a rented Metchosin cabin with his wife and preschool-age daughter needed only a dog to give it perfection.

Anyone can enjoy Metchosin for an afternoon by visiting one of the shoreline parks, among the most beautiful and wild on the south island. Witty's Lagoon, with its sandy beach and view of offshore islets, may be the most popular. Generations have grown up here swimming, picnicking, birdwatching, admiring Sitting Lady Falls on Bilston Creek, exploring the salt marsh and intertidal zone and, more recently, visiting the Witty's Lagoon nature centre. The smaller Albert Head Lagoon Regional Park offers some of the same attractions in a wilder and less travelled setting.

About four kilometres (2.5 miles) inland but easily accessible from the Galloping Goose Trail, Matheson Lake Park is a quiet spot for swimming, fishing, canoeing or picnicking. The trail that loops around the lake makes for a pleasant afternoon walk. Devonian Regional Park gives a good introduction to the Metchosin of long-established farmland as well as untouched wilderness, since its approach lies between farm fields. Riders and walkers share the path down to the cobble beach, where there's a good chance of spotting river otters, seals or orcas as well as a variety of native and migrant birds. The view across Juan de Fuca Strait is of a quiescent volcanic cone: snow-capped Mount Baker in Washington state.

Change is always just down the road, however, even amid all this rural beauty: a 30-hectare (72-acre) parcel for sale in 4-hectare (10 acre) lots, a new subdivision, "for sale" signs and residents muttering into their fairly traded, shade-grown coffee that outsiders and speculators are driving prices beyond the reach of local people. Some newcomers discover that it's not "just like home" and move on, leaving behind the high prices. Yet it's not an uncommon complaint on the south island. It goes with the territory: if you live in paradise, it follows that other people want to as well.

West Coast: Sand, Surf and Liquid Sunshine | 7

A salt tang rides the sea breeze

Right: Birdwatchers can spot the lesser yellowlegs at favourite haunts including Esquimalt Lagoon in Colwood and the Viaduct Flats in Saanich.

Previous pages: Heading home at sunset, a commercial fishboat rounds the tip of the Saanich Peninsula.

Below: Sooke Basin is one of the best natural harbours on the West Coast, but early Hudson's Bay Company traders chose Victoria instead for its good year-round water supply.

out beyond the settled areas of Victoria's urban core and the West Shore communities, where the village of Sooke nestles near tidewater in one of the south island's finest natural harbours. Farther out still, the scattered smaller settlements of Shirley, Point No Point and Jordan River cling to the West Coast Highway, which ends at the fishing community of Port Renfrew on the east bank of the San Juan River.

Some of the region's most gorgeous scenery and favourite destinations lie in these West Coast areas. Urban development hasn't yet caught up with these communities, and, apart from a few remote corners of other municipalities, they are the most rural in the region. Dams in the rolling Sooke Hills gather water for the south island. Unlike other centres, they're separated from Greater Victoria by 50-odd kilometres (about 25 miles) of winding coastal highway that dips and swerves between valley farms, over rocky headlands and along the indented shoreline to the sheltered waters of Sooke Harbour and Sooke Basin.

A Rumble Underfoot

Beneath the lush expanses of forest, fields and malls, the landscape on the West Coast remains as it has been for the past few million years. This area in particular reveals where three terranes, or sections, of the earth's crust collided and overrode each other; with some smaller intrusions from ancient volcanic activity, they built the foundations of modern Vancouver Island.

The igneous and sedimentary Wrangellia Terrane formed far to the south and slammed into western North America about 100 million years ago; the sedimentary Nanaimo Group accumulated along its eastern edge. The volcanic and sedimentary Pacific Rim Terrane ground under Wrangellia about 54 million years ago along the San Juan Fault from near Port Renfrew east to Cobble Hill. The Crescent Terrane—probably a volcanic island—struck it in turn about 42 million years ago along the major Leech River Fault that runs east from Sombrio Point through the remote early gold-mining settlement of Leechtown all the way to Esquimalt Lagoon.

Traces of these ancient events are clearly visible on the earth's surface in West Coast areas. The faults themselves are easiest to pick out from a small plane, as deep creases among the wooded hills, and you can't miss the towers of pillow basalt, part of the volcanic Metchosin Formation, at Sooke Potholes Regional Park.

Large mammals including deer, bears and cougars roam the area, and in remoter areas there have been sightings of wolverines, wolves and elk. Flights of migratory and resident birds, clouds of butterflies and other flying insects, and troops of raccoons, mink and other small mammals inhabit the hillsides and thickets. Occasionally a bear startles a hiker in East Sooke Park or ambles through a clearing beyond Sooke village, but for the most part, wildlife keeps to the safety of the wilderness. In built-up areas humans rarely encounter anything larger than an otter.

First Peoples have a long history here, and many place names have their origins in the earliest times. Sooke draws its name from the T'sou-ke First Nation, which in turn is derived from a Northern Straits Salish word for the

The Roosevelt elk is one of the south island's endangered species.

small, spiny stickleback that inhabits the Sooke River estuary on the Sooke Basin. Two aboriginal groups maintain a strong presence today. Eight small bands of the Scia'new people live at relatively remote Becher Bay in East Sooke, and though their ancestors spoke four different languages, Hul'q'umi'num' is now the main indigenous language of the band's approximately 230 members. The T'Sou-ke First Nation, a few kilometres farther west on the estuary of the Sooke River, numbers just over 220 members and has a vital presence in the nearby town of Sooke.

The T'sou-ke people count their habitation here in thousands of years. According to tradition cited in *That Was Our Way of Life: Memories of Susan Lazzar Johnson, T'Sou-ke Elder,* edited by Kathy Johannesson, long ago the Creator, Sokhalie Tyee, dropped a box on Billings Spit near the mouth of the Sooke River. Out of it climbed four men who became the ancestors of the people of Malahat, Duncan, Elwah (in Washington state) and Sooke.

Since that time, the T'sou-ke people have harvested shellfish and trapped salmon, cut cedars for canoes and bighouses, made baskets from grasses and roots and woven blankets and clothing from mountain goat wool and plant fibres. The land has provided richly for their needs and supported an equally rich culture of dance, song and visual arts.

The T'Sou-ke Nation has also thrown itself into solar-energy generation, becoming one of the most intensively solar-powered communities in Canada. Few could overlook the T'Sou-ke Nation Smart Energy Group's startling slogan: "Providing Environmental Education to Southern Vancouver Island Since 10,000 BCE."

Expanses of glittering solar panels overlie or replace traditional cedar-shake roofs of private homes and community buildings on the reserve. The ambitious 75 kW solar-power project has placed collecting panels on community buildings and homes, creating both off-grid and backup on-grid systems. The clean-energy project reduces the band's energy consumption by up to 30 percent and also produces enough excess power to sell it to BC Hydro. Although other buildings and homes on the south island sport solar panels, the T'sou-ke reserve acts as a showcase of community-based energy production, and the enterprise has attracted the interest of other First Nations throughout BC. T'sou-ke chief Gordon Planes, quoted on the band's website, says, "It's good to be a part of using the gifts that the creator gave us in helping us to take care of Mother Earth. It is now appropriate that First Nations take the lead in demonstrating how to live without fossil fuels once again."

Rich resources also drew the first Europeans to the area. Sooke's first settler in 1849, Captain Walter Grant, described himself as Vancouver Island's first colonist, but the spendthrift gentleman farmer sold in 1851 to a hard-working former HBC coal miner. John Muir and his family built the island's first steam-powered sawmill in 1855 with equipment salvaged from a wrecked steamship and successfully logged the Sooke Basin's towering first-growth timber for the new Victoria market. Other settlers soon followed to develop the area's rich agricultural, forestry, fishery and mineral resources.

Sooke briefly had its own gold rush in 1864, drawing seasoned miners from the Fraser River, Barkerville and farther afield to the Leech River, where the Vancouver Island Exploring Expedition had discovered gold at the junction of the Sooke and Leech rivers. Miners took out an estimated $100,000 worth of gold before the rush and the townsite faded away, but active claims on the stream still produce nuggets.

Any gold rush worth its salt produces at least one mystery, and the Leechtown mystery surrounds a lost tunnel containing gold ingots and Spanish artifacts. The only man who knew its location died in 1959, but that hasn't discouraged treasure seekers. A caution: the Leech River is still fully staked, like other island gold streams, and today claim-jumping is just as likely to get you in serious trouble as it was in the Barkerville days. The real treasure today is the easy six-kilometre (four-mile) walk or cycle up the old railway grade from the Sooke Potholes, a beautiful outing for a warm spring or fall afternoon.

For a community whose name derives from a tiny stickleback fish, Sooke has sprawled over a considerable area: 50 square kilometres (19.3 square miles). Fish and fishing shaped the history of this place as much as logging, mining and farming did. Sooke has long supported both the traditional nets and weirs of aboriginal people and a commercial fishing fleet, and is still a favourite spot to fish offshore in private or rented boats or on fishing charters.

The area draws both local and off-island visitors seeking a day's gourmet or spa outing or a month's wilderness holiday. Among these rocky headlands, stretches of sand and pebble beaches, river mouths and salt marshes, inland forests and meadows, even downtown Sooke is never far from the wilderness.

Today Sooke is no longer a fishing and logging hamlet at the end of a challenging road but a lively, close-knit village centred at the crossroads of the Sooke Road (Highway 14) and Otter Point Road. Outlying housing and condominium developments have sprung up in the surrounding area,

Fly-fishermen cast for trout from a saltwater beach.

Opposite: Sooke Potholes is a cool place for a dip on a sunny summer afternoon. The smooth rock grottos eroded from pillow lava of the ancient seabed.

Top: Whiffin Spit provides a natural barrier to the entrance of Sooke Harbour.

Above: Sooke Harbour House offers world-class gourmet dining to visitors and local residents.

and more are planned. In addition to basic small-town services, Sooke offers bookstores, arts and crafts shops, cafés and a world-class gourmet resort, Sooke Harbour House. Some of Sooke's 10,540 residents still work in resource industries; fishing boats still berth at its docks and logging trucks roll through the town centre. However, more people are involved in local restaurants—favourites are long-established Mom's Café, Nut Pop Thai and Sushi ON the Sea, aboard the docked 24.4-metre (80-foot) gaff-rigged ketch motorsailer *Rolano*—hotels, B&Bs, service businesses, recreation, ecotourism and the arts. Many others run home-based businesses. Change will come now that several large hotel, residential and marina complexes are under construction near the Sooke waterfront, guided by environmentally friendly LEED (Leadership in Energy and Environmental Design) planning.

Hikers, cyclists, kayakers, beachcombers and surfers take advantage of the two big regional parks and a scatter of smaller district parks in the West Coast region. East Sooke Regional Park contains more than 50 kilometres (31 miles) of easy to challenging trails that lead among mixed forests, over rocky ridges and around the coastline with glorious views across Sooke Harbour to the west and out to Juan de Fuca Strait. Picnic spots overlook several coves around the East Sooke peninsula. Also in East Sooke is smaller Roche Cove Park, with trails leading to nearby Matheson Lake Park and connecting with the Galloping Goose Trail.

Sooke Potholes Regional Park is just over 55 hectares (136 acres) in size but stretches for several kilometres along the Sooke River. It contains one of the south island's favourite freshwater swimming spots. The potholes, a series of deep pools carved from the bedrock by glacial action, overflow with cool, clear water spilling from pool to pool near pebble and rock beaches. An adjacent campsite is maintained by The Land Conservancy. The park anchors one end of the Galloping Goose Trail system at the old gold camp of Leechtown.

Whiffin Spit Park, like the Sooke Potholes, has inspired years of local jokes about its unusual name, but it offers spectacular views into Sooke Harbour and across Juan de Fuca Strait south toward Port Angeles in Washington state. It's a beautiful spot for a picnic, birdwatching or an easy beach walk.

Whiffin Spit is also in the backyard of renowned Sooke Harbour House, a favourite south island gourmet and spa getaway. Sooke Harbour House has been welcoming visitors since 1925, originally as an auto camp and tea house. In the hands of Frederique and Sinclair Philip, owners since 1979, it has evolved into a world-class resort that remains mindful of the local people who frequent it for meetings and weddings. Its menu draws on its seasonal kitchen garden and changes daily, the wine list is impressive and the guest bedrooms are beautifully laid out with locally made furniture and the work of island artists.

Beyond Sooke: Surf and Solitude

A classic, sea-swept, wild landscape asserts itself beyond Sooke village as you head west and northwest along the West Coast Highway.

Last-minute hiking supplies are available at Kemp Lake Store, about six kilometres (four miles) west of Sooke. This old-fashioned country store has a friendly café tucked in the back where you can polish off a rib-sticking breakfast or lunch before you venture farther west. On the other hand, you might only get a few kilometres farther along to Tugwell Creek Honey Farm and Meadery and sample the new crop of mead—an ancient Celtic and Teutonic honey wine—or honey from the bee yard. Tugwell Creek was Canada's first meadery, founded in 2003 by owners Dana LeComte and her beekeeper husband, Robert Liptrot.

Top: At French Beach Provincial Park, west of Sooke, visitors can watch grey whales that migrate north every spring and south every fall. Birdwatchers also enjoy the eagles, ospreys and seabirds in the area.

Above: A falling tide reveals pebbles at French Beach.

Many people believe that Muir Creek is a provincial park, perhaps based on the gravel area near its bridge where cars park, but it's private land. Hikers do walk down beside the small estuary to get to the beach of tawny sandstone and grey shingle, an ideal west coast setting for a summer picnic or a well-bundled-up winter walk. At low tide you can spot some of the rare fossils embedded in sandstone ledges, including ancient clams, crabs and snails. The Muir Creek Protection Society, the Dogwood Initiative and other conservation groups are asking the provincial government to protect Muir Creek and its watershed, to ensure a future for the creek's salmon run, first-growth and mature second-growth forest and native plant species.

The main protected shoreline areas between Sooke and Port Renfrew are French Beach and the Juan de Fuca Marine Trail. French Beach Provincial Park is a popular campsite and picnic area. Next door is the much-loved retreat Point No Point, founded in 1952 by Evelyn Packham, a retired nurse. The indomitable Miss Packham operated her few log cabins and served meals to guests and travellers while her property recovered from clear-cut logging, and she established a native plant garden long before most people had any idea what that meant. The name Point No Point may refer to the retreat's point of land, which is actually a separate islet now reachable by a footbridge. Under new owners, the tiny resort now features a fine restaurant and puts up guests in 25 beachside cottages, some with hot tubs and fireplaces and all with spectacular sunset views of Juan de Fuca Strait.

The sandy tidal flats of China Beach invite a shoes-off splash at the waterline.

The tiny settlement of Jordan River, once home to loggers and their families, is well known for the surf that rolls in near the river estuary and the surfers who tirelessly ride the waves there or at nearby China Beach and Sombrio Beach. Jordan River seemed destined to become the site of a huge housing project when the logging company that owned the waterfront and view lands put the property up for sale, but the Capital Regional District (CRD) acquired a large tract of waterfront and forest as future parkland.

China Beach is also a jumping-off point for the 47-kilometre (29-mile) Juan de Fuca Trail, which follows the wild coastline west to Botanical Beach, famous for its rich intertidal life. Hikers use the challenging trail for day hikes or expeditions of several days, especially during the summer. Slides, slope failures and blowdowns can make the route lengthier or more hazardous, especially during the winter or poor weather, so it's important to check local conditions and exercise caution at all times. In addition to China and Botanical beaches, two other trailheads give access to the "moderate to difficult" route: Sombrio Beach and Parkinson Creek.

About three kilometres (two miles) west of Jordan River—no one uses the correct name, River Jordan—China Beach makes an ideal destination for an afternoon on the sandy beach or camping at the drive-in 78-site provincial campground surrounded by mature Douglas fir, Sitka spruce and western red cedar. The steep one-kilometre (0.6-mile) trail down to the beach consists of stairs and a gravel pathway and takes about 20 minutes each way. If you get tired of building sandcastles or wading in the shallows, take a walk west to the pretty waterfall or east to Second Beach.

Spanish navy lieutenant Manuel Quimper named Sombrio River ("sombre/dull river") for its dark ramparts of huge trees misshapen from centuries of hard winds and the pounding waves that foam relentlessly over jagged reefs and rocks and up the sandy beach. For about 30 years Sombrio Beach was home to people who'd built shelters and small houses of driftwood and salvaged materials, but the long-time residents—many of them serious surfers who wanted to live close to the big waves—were evicted in a much-protested campaign in 1997. Today the beach is part of the Juan de Fuca Trail system; the homes have been torn down, and no residents are in evidence, although it's still a popular spot for surfers.

Look but don't touch: even a drop of sunblock lotion in a Botanical Beach tide pool can kill the rich intertidal sea life.

Most of the people passing through Sombrio Beach, at kilometre 29 (mile 18) west of China Beach, are day visitors or hikers walking the Juan de Fuca Trail over a few days or in stages. Parkinson Creek at kilometre 37.6 (mile 23.4) is roughly four kilometres (2.5 miles) from campgrounds at Little Kuitsche Creek to the east and Payzant Creek farther west. Kilometre 47 (mile 29.2) is the final trailhead at Botanical Beach near Port Renfrew.

The profusion of intertidal plants and animals—species of starfish, sea anemones, sea urchins, chitons, barnacles and other colourful inhabitants—and the unusual sculpted sandstone formations make Botanical Beach a special place, especially at low tide when visitors can view the tide pools. In 1901 the rich ecosystem attracted Dr. Josephine Tilden, the University of Minnesota's first female scientist, who founded the West Coast's first marine research station there. It closed a few years later, but other Canadian and American universities still conduct research at Botanical

Beach. Visitors are asked not to leave or remove anything and not to touch the tide pools, since even a little sunscreen can kill the creatures. There's no campground at Botanical Beach, but walk-in wilderness campsites are available to hikers along the Juan de Fuca Trail.

This wild shore is a place of shipwrecks. One of the first recorded was that of the American brig *Cyrus,* carrying lumber from Steilacoom in Washington state, lost December 23, 1858, off Port Renfrew after days of fighting heavy weather; the crew managed to get ashore through the surf. On November 10, 1860, the schooner *D.L. Clinch* was wrecked at Sombrio Point with a cargo of cabinet wood and cranberries en route to San Francisco. The schooner *Dance* went down the same day closer to Jordan River, perhaps caught by the same storm.

On September 9, 1873, the American bark *Revere* struck a reef off Port Renfrew and began to break up. Aboriginal people watching the scene rushed to rescue the passengers and crew, writes James Gibb in *Shipwrecks off Juan de Fuca.* "With little thought for their own lives, the valiant natives formed a human chain in the surf. After frantic struggles in the frigid waters , all of the survivors found themselves on the beach suffering terribly from exposure and hunger. The very next day, the Indians willingly took them to Victoria, B.C. in their canoes, thus completing an unrewarded act of mercy."

Port Renfrew calls itself "the jewel of the West Coast" for a good reason: the peaceful beauty of its location on the inlet of Port San Juan, yet another place named by Spanish explorer Manuel Quimper on his 1790 survey of the West Coast. Port Renfrew was originally called Port San Juan, but changed its name to avoid confusion with the San Juan Islands in Washington state. Today it has roughly 200 residents.

Black bears frequent the wilderness areas adjacent to Victoria. A mother black bear and her cub are better admired from a distance.

Kayaking, canoeing, salmon and halibut fishing, surfing and hiking all draw visitors to the area, but Port Renfrew's biggest attraction may be its strategic location between the Juan de Fuca Trail and the century-old West Coast Trail, first built along the coastline in 1907 as a life-saving trail, where two centuries of shipwrecks outnumbered the inhabitants of many settlements. Here serious hikers head out northwest toward the village of Bamfield at the far end of the 77-kilometre (approximately 48-mile) West Coast Trail or head southeast on the Juan de Fuca Trail. Both trails lay on spectacular views and wildlife viewing, though hikers should keep in mind that they are traversing bear and cougar country.

Port Renfrew marks the end of the road for the West Coast region, but those who'd rather not retrace their steps to more settled centres can drive over the spine of the island on a good road through the town of Lake Cowichan to Duncan and south on the Island Highway over the Malahat Ridge to Victoria. Taking this circle route offers stunning scenery and a leisurely tour of Cowichan Valley wineries, restaurants and arts—but that's another story.

Opposite: The famous tide pools at Botanical Beach draw visitors from around the world.

Sustenance: Caring for the Land

8

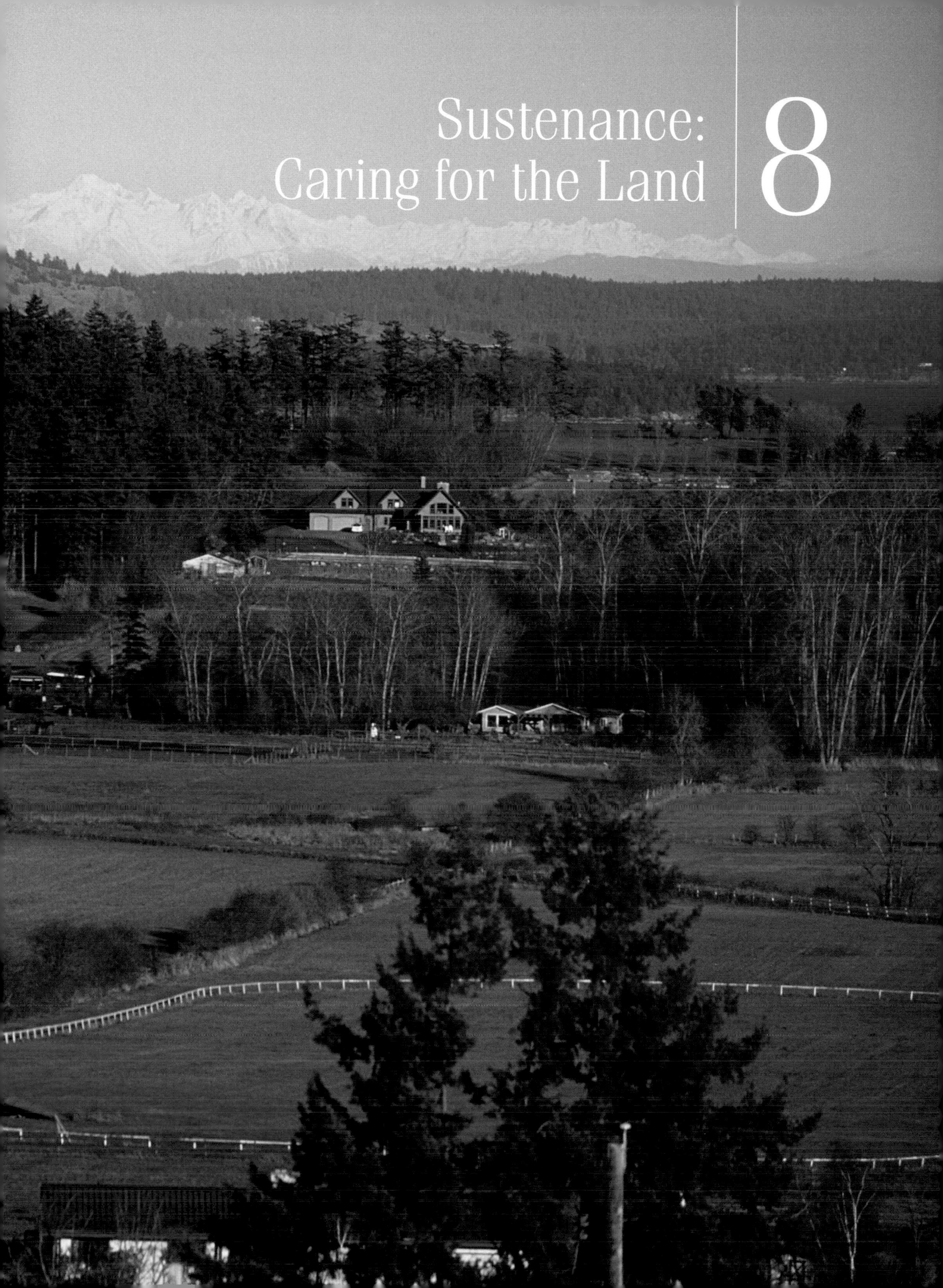

On the sunny garden patio

Right: Will this Metchosin farmer's little piggy ever get to market?

Previous pages: The Saanich Peninsula's patchwork of farm fields feeds the south island.

behind Deep Cove Market in North Saanich, cyclists and walkers pause to sip local apple juice and munch deli sandwiches made with foods grown just down the road. It's easy to see why southern Vancouver Island is a magnet for people who cherish the opportunity to buy or grow natural foods and share their environment with native plants and wildlife.

Deep Cove Market showcases organic foods that are grown, processed and packaged on the Saanich Peninsula, but as exceptional as it is in a world of superstores, it's not unique. Community grocery stores and delis like this one brighten every major centre on the south island—from the Farmer's Daughter in Sooke to The Market on Yates in downtown Victoria to The Root Cellar and the Red Barn Markets in Saanich—sometimes within sight of the fields and orchards that grow their fresh produce. Thrifty Foods and other grocery chains also increasingly feature local produce.

Farm produce at the Moss Street Market makes it easy to eat local.

You'd never guess that just over two centuries ago, a Spanish naval officer noted that this area was useless for agriculture and miserable for human habitation. Even James Douglas, on his 1842 voyage to find a location for a new HBC fur-trade fort—one with strong agricultural potential, year-round fresh water and timber—rejected most of the areas that he visited around the south island.

First Peoples knew better; the land and sea have generously supported their households with fish, meat, vegetables and fruit. The great abundance and variety of foods in turn supported a rich artistic and cultural life. Aboriginal peoples located their villages on good canoe beaches, but they also ventured inland. They hunted deer in the forests and waterfowl in the wetlands, dug starchy camas bulbs in the meadows they cleared with controlled burns and gathered fresh leaves and plant fibres for food, medicine and other domestic needs.

The early English and Scottish settlers who bought HBC land struggled to clear heavily forested slopes for grain and forage crops in a landscape given to rocky outcrops, wetlands and pocket meadows. The elevated central plateau of the Saanich Peninsula offered the largest expanse of relatively level land with good soils, but settlers also took up farming and fruit-growing in Victoria, Esquimalt, Oak Bay, the western communities and Sooke. Most traces of their dairy and beef herds, poultry runs and farm fields have long since vanished, but in quiet byways it's still possible to see big, old grey-barked standard fruit trees or the wild trees that have sprung from their seeds. Overgrown plum, pear and apple trees flank the rail right-of-ways that became the Lochside and Galloping Goose trails. Some may be the last survivors of heritage varieties that are no longer grown; a century and a half later, they still produce small, often late-ripening, fruit that is all the sweeter for being picked from an overhanging branch.

Today's farms are a far cry from the first settlers' few cleared fields among towering evergreens, but they're equally different from the vast, level sections of land under cultivation in other parts of

Native salmonberries ripen in early summer.

Salmon spread on cedar stakes grills beside an open fire at Mungo Martin House in Thunderbird Park in the Royal BC Museum Cultural Precinct.

Harvest one field, plough the next is the farmer's yearly cycle. Pumpkin fields are visible from the Pat Bay Highway in Central Saanich; pick-your-own farms make a fine fall outing.

North America. South island farms are tiny by western Canadian standards; they averaged about 16 hectares (37 acres) in 2001, while in 2006 prairie farms averaged about 473 hectares (1,169 acres) and even BC farms averaged 143 hectares (353 acres). People here will talk straight-faced about a two-hectare farm that a Saskatchewan grain farmer would barely call a garden plot. For all that, our working farms provide a livelihood for market gardeners, greenhouse growers, dairy farmers, stock raisers, organic farmers, turf producers, nursery growers, beekeepers and fruit and nut growers. You can pass examples of most of these in just the three kilometres of Blenkinsop Road north of McKenzie Avenue in Saanich.

Madrona Farm slopes gently down to Blenkinsop Road between two western spurs of Mount Douglas, just outside the park boundary. The upper fields with their rare Garry oak meadow offer a view of the rolling green patchwork of the Blenkinsop Valley and Blenkinsop Lake, which is often veiled in morning mist. One side of the 11-hectare (27-acre) farm was still forested when Ruth and Lawrence Chambers bought it in 1951 and cleared the land to raise cows, vegetables and hay. They were not an average farm couple, even for the mildly eccentric south island: she was an Oxford-educated historian and he was a jack-of-all-trades. But their children had had enough of farming, and after Lawrence's death the fields started to go back to the wild. It took the next generation, grandson David Chambers and his wife, Nathalie, to bring the farm back to life.

Today Madrona Farm rotates through 105 different vegetable crops and 12 cover crops; 35 different fruit varieties grow on 130 new trees that also stabilize the slope. Another 450 newly planted native trees increase the biodiversity, and ponds create important bird habitats. Volunteers do much of the work necessary to produce the vegetables, fruit, eggs and flowers sold to a steady stream of visitors at the farm gate, providing food for about 3,500 households and a

Above: A farmer mechanically harvests silage corn on the Saanich Peninsula.

Left: Herb and mushroom omelette ingredients at Moss Street Market.

surplus donated to food banks. Madrona Farm plays an important role in its community, and in turn has earned the community's admiration and respect.

That's the bright side. A slightly sombre side is perhaps more typical of what happens to small south-island farms. Much of the area's farmland, despite some protection from BC's Agricultural Land Reserve, has been parcelled off and sold as hobby farms or private estates, removing them from food production. As the agricultural land base shrinks and production costs rise, only about 10 percent of Vancouver Island's food supply is grown on-island. When the family group that owned Madrona Farm decided to sell, the farm's operators and The Land Conservancy desperately tried to raise funds to buy the property and maintain it as a working farm. More than 3,000 donors—including 101-year-old Helen and Glenn Sawyer—students, a shopping mall, hotels, restaurants and Victoria Salmon Kings hockey fans put in their dollars to help TLC buy the farm in May 2010. Supporting such efforts, and buying farm-fresh produce, strikes many Victoria area residents as an obligation as well as a pleasure.

Fortunately, many long-time working farms in the region, such as Michell Farms in Saanich, run by the fifth generation of its founding family, have sought out ways to bring the farm experience home to visitors. Every year organizations such as Farm Folk/City Folk, Sooke Region Food CHI Society and the Southern Vancouver Island Growers offer farm tours, usually during the summer or fall. Some tours charge a fee, others are free; they may lay on a meal, fruit tasting, livestock petting, live music or a hayride. Pick-your-own fruit and vegetables, available at some farms, can reduce food costs and give families an interesting afternoon's activity and a glimpse of the farm lifestyle. Look for U-pick pumpkins in October, when pumpkin festivals draw crowds in the weeks before Halloween. At Le Coteau Farms in Saanichton, which specializes mainly in fruit trees and nursery stock, young visitors can enjoy Pumpkin Fest games, corn mazes and a haunted house while their parents sip warm cider and shop the produce stands.

Farm-gate shopping for fresh local foods always makes for a scenic and leisurely outing. Wander the country roads of Metchosin, Sooke, Colwood or the Saanich Peninsula visiting the farm produce and flower stands, or check the Island Farm Fresh online directory of farms (see Resources) if you don't have time to meander. In a single two-kilometre (1.2-mile) stretch of Oldfield Road in Central Saanich, for example, you'll encounter several of the south island's agricultural treasures, including Le Coteau Farms for seasonal vegetables, fruit, fruit trees and nursery plants; Babe's Honey for more sizes, shapes and flavours of honey and beeswax than most people know exist; Sun Wing Greenhouses, offering succulent heritage and market varieties of tomatoes and other fresh vegetables; and Oldfield Orchards, where fresh fruits and vegetables crowd the shelves beside preserves, jams, and home-baked breads and pies. Farm B&Bs around the region introduce guests to farming and the pleasures of country life.

A Cornucopia of Fruits and Flowers

Victoria, famously a city of gardens, has a long-established tradition of garden tours, either self-guided or offered by garden clubs and commercial tour operators. As well as world-renowned, gorgeously landscaped commercial gardens such as the Butchart Gardens in Central Saanich, visitors are free to wander smaller gardens run by municipalities or small businesses, some of them staffed by volunteers. (See Resources.) Beacon Hill Park, the University of Victoria's Finnerty Gardens and the kitchen garden at Sooke Harbour House are some of the best known, but the Oak Bay Native Plant Garden—a small, shady gem on Beach Drive—is also worth a visit.

Less showy but striking in their own way are the community or allotment gardens inspired years ago by Britain's wartime Victory Gardens. People will wait years for a plot and, once they get one, display impressive gardening skills; all summer the community gardens in several municipalities produce a cornucopia of mouth-watering fruits and vegetables and spectacular flowers. As

Apple blossoms brighten a south island orchard.

A border collie competes at the annual Metchosin sheepdog trials.

they approach the city, visitors arriving from the airport or the peninsula ferry terminals can look to the right and see the large, east-sloping Saanich community garden.

Seasonal in harmony with the growing year, excellent plant nurseries abound in almost every corner of the south island. Serving beginner gardeners, professional landscapers and Victoria's many passionate and well-informed home gardeners, they range from small roadside stands offering a few seedlings or bedding plants to large dedicated nurseries staffed by trained horticulturists. The largest offer a vast selection of garden plants, ornaments and tools, while others specialize in plants as diverse as pond plants, rhododendrons, native-plant cultivars or bonsai.

Farmers' markets, about a dozen of them, take over streets or parking lots for one day or evening a week, typically from May through September. Gathering from 10 to 200 vendors—the number and selection will vary every week and by location—most sell not only fresh local fruits and vegetables but flowers, honey, baked goods, preserves, meats and dairy products. Soaps, clothing, leather goods, walking sticks, bed linens and jewellery are available at the larger markets in Metchosin, on Moss Street in Victoria, on the Saanich Peninsula and in Sidney (see Resources for BC Association of Farmers' Markets website).

It's not only the mild winters, long slow springs and autumns and sunny summers, it's also the generous mixture of people from all over the world that has made southern Vancouver Island the specialty-product destination of western Canada. Local people produce a head-turning list of fruits, vegetables, baked goods, meats, cheeses, specialty items, beers and wines. Delicacies or staples, they mainly come from small producers scattered around the rural parts of the Victoria region, and they offer scenic outings and opportunities to sample new and unusual foods. Wine, mead, cider and beer tastings are a pleasure year-round, and draw people from both far afield and just down the road. You can also pick up local products at many liquor stores. South island vineyards, orchards, bee yards and farms raise produce that often goes straight into their own fermenting vats for transformation into alcoholic and non alcoholic beverages. Many are winning prizes and gaining stellar reputations far beyond the island.

A handful of small, mostly family-operated, wineries take advantage of the sunshine and sloping glacial soils on the Saanich Peninsula. Muse, Starling Lane and Winchester offer wine tastings and tours—meals or gift shops may also be available—but it's best to check current availability and opening days before hitting the road.

Top: Fireweed honey in the making.

Above: Sooke Harbour House has its own small bee yard.

A taxi or limousine service can get you there in style if you don't have a designated driver. An afternoon of cycling would get you to several cellars; the wineries lie among their vineyards within the northern 15 kilometres (nine miles) of the peninsula, from Old West Saanich Road to Deep Cove, or you can savour each cellar at your leisure on successive days.

Island beekeepers have set out their hives in the Sooke area for many years, taking advantage of the plentiful summer bloom of wildflowers, especially pink-blossomed fireweed that colonizes recently burned or cleared areas. Beekeeping is year-round work for modest profits, and the smallest setback can easily make it a labour of love rather than a livelihood. Dana LeComte and her husband, Bob Liptrot, discovered that after a few years of keeping bees at Tugwell Creek, near Sooke, and opted for a better way to use their own and their bees' resources: brewing an ancient honey wine, mead. Tugwell Creek Meadery now produces several oak-aged meads—sweet or dry, some flavoured with currants, blackberries or other local fruit—and of course liquid honey, candles, bars of beeswax and honey in the comb.

Beer has been a Victoria specialty right from the days when Vancouver Island was a colony. One of the 19th-century brews was Phoenix Export Lager (the old brewery sign is on display in the old town exhibit of the Royal BC Museum). In 2003 the Phoenix name was revived by one of the latest generation of Victoria microbreweries, Phillips Brewing Co., which produces half a dozen other highly rated beers, ales and porters. Phillips is just one of about eight craft breweries, several of them associated with gastro brewpubs, now producing dozens of different brews from traditional to novelty on the south island. Among other popular breweries are Spinnakers, Lighthouse and Swans Buckerfields, all making small batches with natural processes and as many local ingredients as possible. In turn they provide the waste products of brewing to farmers for nutritious livestock feed. Beer tours may not be as readily available as wine tours—maybe because some beer aficionados would still rather take on a pub crawl than a tony-sounding beer tasting—but local breweries can provide details on upcoming tastings or tours (see Resources). Then sit back and enjoy the remarkably varied flavours of these new ventures into an age-old craft.

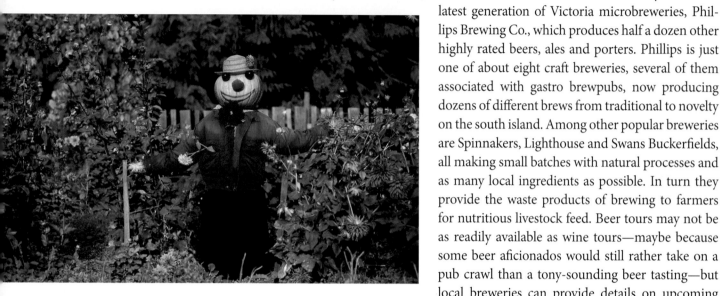

Not every pumpkin becomes a pie or jack-o'-lantern. A pumpkin-headed scarecrow guards a Central Saanich flower garden.

A landscape quilted with apple orchards going back a century and a half is a natural place to set a cidery, and if the ciderhouse overlooks its own orchards and fields to the blue haze of the Strait of Georgia, so much the better. Sea Cider is a relatively new enterprise on the Saanich Peninsula, where owners Bruce and Kristen Jordan have planted their own orchard but also buy quality fruit from local growers, whether they have one tree or a hundred. Their apple ciders and perry (pear cider) are available in liquor stores, but who wouldn't rather relax with a sparkling glass and a tasting platter while enjoying the view?

Green Living

South island producers, from traditional farmers to innovative specialty-crop growers or vintners, work hard to conserve natural resources and protect the environment we share. Newcomers sometimes overlook or underestimate this quiet passion for green living and stewardship on the part of ordinary people of all tastes and backgrounds. It's not something to trifle with, this dedication to living lightly on the land and sharing its resources with wildlife and native plants. The person who takes you to task for tossing a wrapper or idling your car for too long may not be a wild-eyed protester but a spry granny wielding an umbrella. Don't push your luck; she probably ran a marathon last week and holds a black belt in something dangerous.

South islanders care seriously about their environs. They're keenly aware that they inhabit one of the world's most spectacular landscapes and most liveable cities. The regional population is projected to grow by roughly 40 percent by 2036, increasing the pressure on resources of every kind.

The south island's area is sharply finite, limited by the Malahat Ridge to the north and the sea in every other direction, with equally limited fresh water and other resources. Victoria will face the highest density, and inevitably developers will push to open up ALR-protected land in outlying areas. Early logging stripped much of the West Shore, West Coast and Saanich Peninsula, pollution has damaged beaches and waterways, and water resources are strained every summer. Residential and industrial development, recreation and introduced plants and animals threaten native species.

Natural beauty is what has drawn most people to the region, from the first aboriginal peoples to today's wide-eyed newcomers just stepping off the ferry; no one wants to lose this beauty to an asphalt-and-cement wasteland or dreary condominium tracts. Yet developments like the new golf resort and subdivisions in Langford proceeded despite protests from First Peoples, ecoactivists and local residents.

Solutions lie close to home. Even without stepping out of their own backyards, residents can (and do) help in re-greening the land: they can eat local products, reduce water and electricity use, avoid harsh household and garden chemicals, plant butterfly- or bird-friendly gardens, plant trees, plant native species, and instead of powerboating or driving ATVs, consider ecofriendly outdoor activities such as birdwatching, hiking or kayaking.

Many conservation, outdoor and historical groups are active on the south island, and most regularly seek members and volunteers. Clearing a stream bed, excavating an early settlement, planting Garry oak seedlings or guiding visitors at a heritage site not only serves the community, it's also a good way to learn local and natural history, get a workout and meet new friends.

"A city of villages" is a description often given to London and other large cities, but it's equally true of the Victoria region, with numerous community groups and projects. Many are profoundly connected with the natural world, though not always in obvious ways. People who grow flowers or produce for their stalls at weekly farmers' markets are as likely as not to be organic farmers, and stores that sell natural foods or conservation-oriented wares—including the Red Barn, Lifestyle Markets, Planet Organic and the Green Village Eco Store in Sidney—are booming. So is the Organic Islands festival held in July at Glendale Gardens; its slogan is "Live green. Buy local. We'll show you how." Musicians, organizers and concert-goers pass the hat for local conservation efforts or international relief. Artists and artisans seek out "rescued" or recycled materials to produce provocative works. Conservation has not only gone public, it's become hip and fun.

Wild-caught, British Columbia prawns are deemed a "Best Choice" by organizations that monitor seafood sustainability.

Discovery: Things to See and Do

A carriage tour of James Bay passes the Parliament Buildings.

Previous pages: Victoria hosts a Tall Ships Festival every second year in the Inner Harbour. Watch for the mock naval battles off Beacon Hill Park.

BC Ferries vessels pass each other off Swartz Bay. The smaller ferry is bound for the Gulf Islands, and the larger one serves the Swartz Bay–Tsawwassen run.

Live on southern Vancouver Island for a lifetime and you might just scratch the surface of what there is to do and see in the region. Newcomers and visitors who've never before set foot on the island often put Vancouver Island natives to shame, telling us of interesting places and activities right down the road.

Victoria and its region offer pleasures ranging from an afternoon's intensive shopping to a week's leisurely retreat on a wild beach frequented mostly by shorebirds and otters. You can explore dozens of parks and trails, educate yourself on anything from environmental studies to ancient languages, arrange for a massage or a palm reading, sign up for wilderness or urban tours, sail on a square-rigger, travel by pedicab or horse-drawn carriage, take in music from opera to rock and eat freshly grown local foods used in a score of world cuisines.

Getting to the Victoria Region

If you're planning a visit, you can get here from off-island by sea or by air and from up-island by car, bus or train. Four different ferry companies and a changing number of cruise operators serve the island from Tsawwassen on BC's Lower Mainland and from Seattle, Port Angeles and Anacortes in northwestern Washington state in the USA. Commercial and private airplanes fly into the Victoria International Airport in North Saanich, and seaplanes land in Victoria's Inner Harbour—one of Canada's busiest air routes is from there to Vancouver Harbour—or at a float base near the airport. Helicopters use either the airport or a helipad at Ogden Point near the entrance to the Inner Harbour. You can also charter an airplane or a boat to carry you to the south island or pilot your own boat or plane. On a clear day, any route will take you among the photogenic Gulf Islands or through other scenic areas. Ferry captains frequently stop to allow passengers a good view of passing porpoises, orcas or other wildlife.

BC Ferries
(250) 381-1401 (Victoria head office)
1-888-223-3779 (toll-free in North America)
www.bcferries.com

Black Ball Ferry Line
(250) 386-2202 (Victoria) • (360) 457-4491 (Port Angeles)
www.cohoferry.com

Victoria Clipper
(250) 382-8100 • 1-800-888-2535 (toll-free)
www.clippervacations.com

Washington State Ferries
(206) 464-6400 (Seattle)
www.wsdot.wa.gov/ferries

West Coast Trail Express (buses from Victoria and other points to the trailheads of the West Coast Trail and the Juan de Fuca Trail)
(250) 477-8700 (Victoria) • 1-888-999-2288 (toll-free in Canada)
www.trailbus.com

VIA Rail Canada (passenger trains between Victoria and Courtenay)
1-888-VIA-RAIL • 1-888-842-7245 (toll-free)
www.viarail.ca

Canada Customs
1-800-461-9999 (toll-free in Canada)
(204) 983-3500 • (506) 636-5064 (outside Canada)
www.cbsa-asfc.gc.ca

Greyhound Canada
(250) 388-5248 (Victoria)
1-800-661-TRIP • 1-800-661-8747 (toll-free)

Travel agencies can provide information on major airlines that serve Victoria, but here's a sampling:

Air Canada
1-888-247-2262 (toll-free)
www.aircanada.com

Harbour Air Seaplanes
(250) 384-2215 (Victoria)
1-800-665-0212 (toll-free in North America)
www.harbourair.com

HeliJet
(250) 386-7676 (Victoria) • 1-800-665-4354 (toll-free)
www.helijet.com

Pacific Coastal Airlines
(250) 655-6411 (Victoria) • 1-800-663-2872 (toll-free)
www.pacificcoastal.com

WestJet
1-800-538-5696 (toll-free)
www.westjet.com

A seaplane touches down in the Inner Harbour off Fisherman's Wharf.

Finlayson Arm reflects the last sunset light seen from the Malahat Drive summit.

Visiting the Victoria Region

More than three million people visit Victoria and area every year. Fortunately accommodation is available to suit every taste and budget, from luxury hotels to modest backpackers' hostels. In addition to staying in conventional hotels, motels and B&Bs, you can rent a cottage or cabin, camp in a tent or RV or stay on a houseboat. Services range from luxury spa treatment to bare-bones housekeeping rentals, with every possible variation in between. Be sure to learn what's being provided and any special charges before you head out.

The south island's popularity makes it a relatively expensive place to visit. An online booking service or a travel agent can match you with the right accommodations, but here are some places to start:

Tourism British Columbia
(250) 356-6363 (Victoria)
1-800-HELLOBC • 1-800-435-5622 (toll-free)
www.hellobc.com
(For camping information, search under Accommodations for Victoria and area)

Tourism Victoria
(250) 953-2033 (Victoria) • 1-800-663-3883 (toll-free)
www.tourismvictoria.com

British Columbia Lodging and Campgrounds Association
www.camping.bc.ca

BC Parks Campground Reservations
1-800-689-9025 (toll-free) • 1-519-826-6850 (international)
http://www.env.gov.bc.ca/bcparks/reserve/

See next page for a list of Victoria and region's best-known hotels, inns and resorts.

Victoria's famous hanging baskets decorate downtown lamp posts.

Staying in the Victoria Region

A visitor falls in love with Victoria, goes home, packs up and moves here permanently: it's a common story. Countless Victoria area residents came here for a holiday or a short work stay, and are still here decades later. Others arrive with their goods and chattels, only to find that this wasn't their city of dreams after all. It's an expensive cure, but a little advance research and planning can spare you any grief. A number of apartment hotels, short-term rentals and house-exchange services cater to people who want to test the waters before they leap in.

You can investigate some of these options online:

British Columbia Travel Guide: Victoria Home Rentals
www.bctravel.com/rentbc/victoria-home-rentals.html

Victoria Home Exchange
www.4homex.com/1victoriahomeexchange.htm

For longer-term rentals, to buy a home or to find a real estate agent:

Victoria Real Estate Board
www.vreb.org

VICTORIA'S BEST-KNOWN GUEST ACCOMMODATIONS

Fairmont Empress Hotel
Victoria's renowned downtown hotel; fine accommodation and dining overlooking the Inner Harbour, famous for its pricey but memorable high tea.
(250) 384-8111
1-866-540-4429 (toll-free)
www.fairmont.com/Empress

Union Club
Rooms and excellent meals in a traditional businessperson's club in the heart of town, overlooking the Inner Harbour.
(250) 384-1151
www.unionclub.com

Inn at Laurel Point
Hotel overlooking the Inner Harbour and Esquimalt Harbour, a few minutes' stroll from downtown.
(250) 386-8721
1-800-663-7667 (toll-free)
www.laurelpoint.com

Ocean Island Backpackers' Inn
Friendly, funky and fun downtown accommodation at a range of affordable prices.
(250) 385-1788 or (250) 385-1789
1-888-888-4180 (toll-free)
www.oceanisland.com

English Inn
A traditional inn located in Esquimalt, with rooms and a beautiful garden setting.
(250) 388-4353
1-866-388-4353 (toll-free)
www.englishinn.ca

Oak Bay Guest House
Upscale, English-inspired B&B in a beautiful setting close to charming shops and pleasant walks.
(250) 598-3812
1-800-575-3812 (toll-free)
www.oakbayguesthouse.com

Oak Bay Beach Hotel
(reopening in 2011)
Waterfront hotel with unequalled views from a park-like property on the Oak Bay foreshore.
1-800-668-7758 (toll-free)
www.oakbaybeachhotel.com

Brentwood Bay Lodge
Kayak from the front dock of this Central Saanich waterfront hotel; West Coast gourmet meals are served in the modern dining room.
(250) 544-2079
1-888-544-2079 (toll-free)
www.brentwoodbaylodge.com

Sidney Pier Hotel
New multi-storey hotel on Sidney's waterfront with view rooms, a spa and fine dining; the site of the Shaw Ocean Discovery Centre, an aquarium and marine education facility.
(250) 655-9445
1-866-659-9445 (toll-free)
www.sidneypier.com

Westin Bear Mountain Resort
Golfer's paradise in Langford with rooms, fine dining and two courses designed by Jack Nicklaus.
(250) 391-7160
1-888-533-2327 (toll-free)
www.bearmountain.ca

Sooke Harbour House
Waterfront inn 45 minutes west of downtown Victoria, popular with residents and visitors for its gourmet dining and view rooms.
(250) 642-3421
1-800-889-9688 (toll-free)
www.sookeharbourhouse.com

Point No Point Resort
Waterfront cabins and restaurant set amongst towering cedars and firs on a wild West Coast beach.
(250) 646-2020
www.pointnopointresort.com

B&B in Victorian style.

Above: Abkhazi Garden, the backyard legacy of Princess Peggy and Prince Nicholas Abkhazi, was saved from development and is now part of The Land Conservancy of BC.

Top right: Dzonoqua and her baby on a totem pole at Mungo Martin House.

Seasonal Delights

The mild, sunny climate of the Victoria region makes it a wonderful place to explore in any season. The perennial pleasures, of course, revolve around the south island's rich cultural landscape, which features music from renaissance and classical to punk, several professional theatre companies and a modest club scene. Another year-round draw is the shopping, whether that means fascinating trinkets from Fan Tan Alley, chic one-off fashion from boutiques on LoJo—Lower Johnson Street—or fine woollens, linens, porcelain and crystal from Government Street.

Newcomers sometimes complain that there are no seasons here—one reason for the dismissive tag "Lotusland"—but maybe they're deceived by the beaches and palm trees. The seasons are all present and accounted for; they just don't match up with the long winters and rapid-fire springs and summers of colder climates.

Our south island spring is a long, slow process of reawakening as the earth warms and offshore breezes tease the coastline. Willow buds don't pop open in a day here but take weeks to display their pussy-willow fuzz. Muddy rivulets spring from the ground, making footpaths and bike trails mushy underfoot for a month or so as new growth probes up between last fall's dead leaves into the light of day.

Here spring blossoms are famously showy, especially the cloudbanks of pink and white on ornamental cherry and plum trees. The display may not be a deeply rooted cultural institution like sakura time in Japan, but it draws increasing numbers of visitors from snowbound regions of western Canada and the western states. It's a time to take leisurely walks in the tentative warmth and fitful sunshine under high, pale spring skies. Children of all ages fly kites at Beacon Hill Park, Gyro Park on Cadboro Bay, Swan Lake or any green space that's relatively free of power lines and trees. Hardy souls may take their first saltwater dip or break out the kayak or canoe for a brisk paddle—though real diehards will have splashed right through the winter—and start investigating the bedding plants at local nurseries. Migrant birds flock through the area, and birdwatchers, in quiet pursuit, also show their colours. Training becomes more intense on rugby and soccer pitches and the hopeful turn out to watch practices at Beacon Hill Park's cricket pitch well in advance of the season.

Things to do in the spring:

- walk through a residential neighbourhood where snowdrops, crocuses, daffodils, hyacinths and tulips are starting to push up through the soil; enjoy the masses of ornamental cherry and plum blossoms on boulevard and backyard trees
- visit Beacon Hill Park, where flowers and trees from all over the world bloom, along with an estimated two million native, blue-flowered camas plants
- play golf on some of the region's dozen-plus public and private golf courses on a mild January day, then send postcards to your snowbound friends in colder climes
- take a marine wildlife tour to see seals, sea lions, marine birds and occasionally whales
- join an organized tour of public or private gardens, such as the Butchart Gardens
- luxuriate in a hotel spa while rain lashes the windows on a grey afternoon
- visit the Pacific Undersea Gardens to meet an octopus or shark nose to nose through a plate-glass window
- attend a service or take a quiet walk through St. Andrew's Cathedral (Roman Catholic; beautiful stained glass, altar furnishings by local aboriginal artists Charles Elliott and Roy Henry Vickers), Christ Church Cathedral (Anglican; look for the stone dove on the pillar), St. Andrew's Presbyterian Church (brilliant acoustics) or St. Paul's Anglican Church (one of the oldest in BC); check times and visitor policies for churches, synagogues, temples and meeting houses of various faiths
- break out an umbrella and walk in the rain; you don't have to shovel it
- attend a nature program at one of the Capital Regional District regional parks; most are inexpensive or free, and many welcome children; check first for registration information and other details
- watch the Swiftsure International Yacht Race in late May
- go surfing at Jordan River or another West Coast beach; you can rent surfing equipment in Victoria and possibly in Sooke, but not at the beaches
- bundle up and take a walk on China Beach, watching for migrating grey whales offshore

Nick Howard carves at the Royal BC Museum.

Summer often arrives with one scorching day that sends people digging for their inner tubes and water noodles and scurrying to the lakes and ocean beaches. Hot weather can stretch blissfully through month after month of sunny days, with maybe the occasional rainy patch, and real Victorians stick around to enjoy it. Why travel anywhere else when it's so gorgeous here?

Things to do in the summer:

- rent a kayak or join a guided tour for a scenic paddle around the historic Inner Harbour; stay near the shoreline to avoid mid-harbour seaplane landings and takeoffs
- take a whale-watching boat tour from Victoria, Sidney, Sooke or another south island port
- throw yourself into Victoria's Ska Fest in July for performances and workshops in ska, reggae, jazz, Latin, rock and more; it's a huge Victoria tradition that's definitely not only for ska kids, since hippies, punks, skaters, emo kids and surfers all come out in force—look for great tattoos and crazy fashion sense
- travel to the Centre of the Universe interpretive centre at the Dominion Astrophysical Observatory to enjoy the interactive displays and stargaze through telescopes provided by Royal Astronomical Society of Canada volunteers

- watch the water ballet in the Inner Harbour at 10:45 on Sunday mornings from May to September, when five Harbour ferry skippers dance their boats to the "Blue Danube Waltz"; turn up early for a good spot on the causeway

- study the artists at work during the Moss Street Paint-In, the largest outdoor visual arts event on Vancouver Island, in July

- hike or bike along the waterfront from the Inner Harbour through Beacon Hill Park, east toward Oak Bay and Saanich or west toward Esquimalt and the West Shore, and explore some of the area's scores of large and small parks; check first that cyclists are allowed, since some trails are for walkers only

- take in the daily summer arts and crafts market in Bastion Square or one of many weekly farmers' markets in the region, where you'll find fresh produce and flowers as well as bread, preserves, soaps, clothing, pottery, jewellery, clothing, walking sticks and anything else a vendor might turn up with

- become a citizen of Rifflandia for the major music festival's September "mash-up of amazing music and local lifestyle," considered the hippest thing happening in Victoria right now and slickly organized with both international and local talent from the independent music scene; line up early—Rifflandia is a popular gig for bands and fans

- join a walking tour or an evening ghost walk to learn the remarkable history of downtown Victoria's buildings and public spaces

- come out for Victoria Pride Week in late June, which culminates with the Pride Parade, to celebrate the gay and lesbian community

- enjoy one of the seasonal festivals: the Luxton Rodeo in Langford in late May; Victoria's JazzFest and the Oak Bay Tea Party in June; the floating Symphony Splash concert at Victoria's Inner Harbour on the August long weekend; the dramatic Fringe Festival in August and September

- re-enact bygone days at restored Fort Rodd Hill and adjacent Fisgard Lighthouse; check for dates and times of military and other re-enactment events

Kayakers take in the sights of the Inner Harbour.

Marine wildlife tours offer a chance of an up-close look at seals, sea lions, marine birds and, occasionally, whales.

The first few leaves drift to the ground almost unnoticed as the warm days of early fall linger but grow shorter. Late fall makes up for its damp chill and gloomy mornings by remaining shamelessly beautiful. The last blackberries hang temptingly out of reach of all but birds. Silvery dew jewels the grass and leaves until midmorning, and the broadleaf maples and alders turn to beaten copper and bronze before their leaves whirl away in the first fall storm. Gardeners rake leaves and turn the soil where their flowers bloomed only weeks ago. Families tour the bright pumpkin fields to choose the best jack-o'-lanterns. Pumpkin-coloured school buses trundle around their routes. Harbour ferries tie up for the season and skateboarders wear toques.

Things to do in the fall:

- attend the Classic Boat Show, Luxton Fall Fair or Saanich Fall Fair on Labour Day weekend
- stock up the larder at farm-gate market stands, especially in rural areas of the Saanich Peninsula and the West Shore, where you'll find eggs, honey, vegetables, flowers, baked goods, candy and country crafts
- take in Greek Fest in early September; enjoy the dancing and presentations, but especially enjoy the authentic food prepared by members of Victoria's active Greek community
- pick your own jack-o'-lantern or pie pumpkin from the fields at the bottom of Cordwood Hill in Central Saanich or at one of many other farms, and try your luck at getting through a corn maze
- watch the salmon spawn in the Goldstream River at Goldstream Provincial Park, a time-honoured south-island tradition in September; some of the spawning fish were raised and released by local schoolchildren
- take a walk up Antique Row on Fort Street to admire everything from 1950s magazines to fine furniture pieces that came around the Horn under sail to Victoria in the 1850s
- attend a Remembrance Day service in any community; Victoria's is the largest, but Esquimalt and Sidney also get a good turnout because of their military bases
- have a fall picnic on China Beach, watching for migrating grey whales offshore
- plan a heritage apple tasting day, visiting Saanich Peninsula and West Shore fruit farms

War memorial, Parliament Buildings.

Winter offers the exciting prospect of a snow day or two. Kids rush to dust off their toboggans, and their elders' hilariously inept driving makes the roads a terror—or maybe there'll just be grey drizzle that falls softly from the fragrant firs and cedars. Tramping through the woods in pursuit of windfall greenery for Christmas wreaths and combing shops for the perfect gift take our minds off the dwindling year.

Things to do in the winter:

- take part in wine, beer, cider and mead tastings, mainly in the rural Saanich Peninsula, West Shore or West Coast, to sample some of the south island's award-winning offerings; some producers feature not only tastings but also gift shops and gourmet meals
- tour the Parliament Buildings—Legislative Buildings, to those who forget Vancouver Island was once a colony in its own right—and sit in the public gallery if the Legislative Assembly is sitting; prepare to take cover, since BC politics can get scrappy
- stake out a bench in Victoria Butterfly Gardens some rainy winter day to enjoy the tropical warmth and to watch the brilliant flying creatures flit through the indoor jungle
- wheedle your way into a Robbie Burns dinner on January 25; these are held by the private Union Club, Royal Canadian Legions and other associations; if you succeed, the ploughboy poet would be proud of you

Shaw Ocean Discovery Centre in Sidney is an aquarium and marine education facility.

A crab pot dropped into inshore waters may resurface with a mess of Dungeness crabs for supper.

- visit the arts and crafts shows scheduled in almost every municipality in November and December; the south island supports large numbers of artists and artisans including bookbinders, potters, jewellers, weavers, woodcarvers, fabric artists, sculptors, glassblowers, printmakers and painters
- take a hayride on a Saanich Peninsula or West Shore farm; the rides are often followed by a meal
- attend a Victoria Symphony or choir performance of the classics; each year, several groups stage Handel's *Messiah*, Tchaikovsky's *The Nutcracker Suite* and other seasonal favourites
- make your own music by getting out and carolling with friends or a choir
- take a horse-drawn carriage ride in the snow or misty rain, then warm up with wine or a toddy at a historic neighbourhood pub like Four Mile House in View Royal or the Prairie Inn in Saanichton
- watch Sidney's Lighted Sail Past of local and visiting boats in December from a shoreline park and warm up in a waterfront restaurant
- visit the Butchart Gardens once they are decorated with holiday lights that turn an already beautiful place into a magical realm; the gift shop is a great spot to find garden- and outdoors-related presents
- take in the Lion Dance and other week-long festivities of Chinese New Year celebrations in late February

For the Young and Young At Heart:

- Downtown, the young and hip hang out on Lower Johnson Street, or in Fernwood; each has a vibrant community. Sample the excellent lunches and sweets at Murchie's Tea & Coffee on Government Street, and go for broke at the discount tables next door at Munro's Books. Get a trim at Lab Salon on Lower Johnson or a tattoo at Pair O' Dice across the street or Urge on Cook Street. Try the Mexican food at Mo:Lé on Johnson Street.

- Street Level Espresso on Fort Street, run by a connoisseur of cameras as well as coffee, is tiny, very good and full of interesting things. They sell Lomo cameras and loads of independent photo magazines; browse over a memorable coffee.

- Pluto's Restaurant on Cook Street looks like a 1950s drive-in with funky extraterrestrial decor. The big overhead doors from its garage days still work, which makes this a place to be on hot summer evenings. Great burgers and milkshakes, daily specials, friendly staff and live music on weekends.

- Ditch Records on Johnson Street has an excellent selection of both vinyl records and CDs, especially of the indie or little-known sort. A quick question here will turn up the best—or at least coolest—shows in the city for the next month, and they'll probably sell you tickets. Lyle's Place on Yates Street sells records, posters and tickets and rents DVDs. The Turntable in Fan Tan Alley specializes in vintage vinyl of every kind.

- Vic West Skatepark on Esquimalt Road at Bay Street, Ted De Gros wrote, "has more than just something for everyone, it has 100 things for each different skater." Try out your kickflip or krooked grind or just hang with friends at one of Canada's biggest and slickest skateparks.

A skater flies high at Vic West.

- The Noodle Box on Fisgard Street prepares delicious cooked-to-order Asian fusion noodles with a wide selection of sauces and toppings in cardboard cartons. Expect to wait for your takeout or one of the few tables; this is a favourite lunch or dinner spot. A newer location on Douglas Street near the Empress has more sit-down space.

- Pick up a flexible 4on4 Sportspak of tickets to watch the Victoria Seals (Golden Baseball League), Victoria Rebels (Canadian Junior Football League), Victoria Shamrocks (Senior A Box Lacrosse) and Victoria Highlanders (United Soccer Leagues); the general admission tickets are for four regular-season games or for four people to attend any one game. Tickets to the Salmon Kings (East Coast Hockey League) are also available in mini packs and season ticket packages.

- Who's playing where? To find out, take a quick walk downtown and read the current band posters on windows, walls and poles. Some of Victoria's best drinking spots are also the best music venues. All of them are fairly sticky-floor-standing-room-only, and none allow minors, but great indie bands come through the smaller venues and tickets are rarely more than $25: look into Lucky Bar on Yates Street, Logan's Pub on Cook Street and the nightclubs Sugar on Yates Street, Element on Douglas Street and Evolution on Discovery Street.

Discovering the Victoria Region in One Day, Three Days or One Week

Visitors come to Victoria for anything from a whirlwind afternoon to a leisurely few weeks. Whatever time is available will feel too short to explore the entire south island, but here are some suggestions for what you can realistically see in one day, three days or a week, starting from the Inner Harbour and working outward. Turn up with comfortable walking shoes, a tote bag or day pack for needs and desires, and, if a sprinkle of H$_2$O would spoil your day, an umbrella.

One day:

- stroll along the lower causeway of the Inner Harbour, where many artists and artisans display their handiwork; some create art as you watch
- walk from the Inner Harbour up Government Street, window-shop the many import and art shops, have lunch in Chinatown on Fisgard Street and walk back down to the harbour along Wharf Street
- visit the Royal BC Museum and the National Geographic IMAX Theatre at the corner of Government and Bellevue streets
- sip afternoon tea at the Empress or the James Bay Tea Room; note that high tea is usually a full meal of sandwiches, scones and pastries
- take a horse-drawn carriage ride or Tally-Ho ride (20 minutes to over an hour) through the historic James Bay neighbourhood, along the waterfront or through Beacon Hill Park

Three days, add:

- join a kayak or Victoria Harbour Ferry tour of the historic Inner Harbour
- stroll out to the end of the Ogden Point breakwater at the entrance to Victoria Harbour
- walk in Beacon Hill Park and James Bay, stopping for flavoured soft ice cream or a snack at Victoria's cherished Beacon Drive-In or a quiet meal at Heron Rock Bistro or the Ogden Point Café, with its view of Victoria's shipping lanes
- visit Capital Iron on Store Street, a one-of-a-kind Victoria emporium that evolved from war surplus marine sales into a department store where two heritage brick buildings and an outdoor enclosure overflow with outdoor, marine, workshop, home and garden supplies

- take children of all ages to the Victoria Bug Zoo, the Crystal Pool, Family Fun Park in Langford or one of many local playgrounds and beaches
- drive or join a tour to the renowned Butchart Gardens, where you can amble through the spectacular gardenscapes reclaimed over the years from a former limestone quarry, and eat in the café or restaurant; in winter enjoy the fairyland of seasonal lights and tableaux, and on summer Saturday evenings watch the closing fireworks
- hear live jazz, blues, folk or other music in downtown nightclubs
- visit the Maritime Museum of BC in Victoria's original courthouse in Bastion Square, Emily Carr House in James Bay, the BC Aviation Museum near Sidney, the CFB Esquimalt Naval and Military Museum, Craigflower Farm or another of the area's many excellent museums
- hop onto a Victoria Harbour Ferry at the Inner Harbour dock and hop off at Fisherman's Wharf for lunch at Barb's Fish and Chips, at historic Point Ellice House for a tour and traditional afternoon tea or at Songhees for a meal at Spinnakers Brewpub; a longer trip will give you a thorough harbour tour with a running commentary on local history

One week, add:

- visit the Centre of the Universe and the Herzberg Institute (Dominion Astrophysical Observatory) on Little Saanich Mountain; dress warmly for stargazing with volunteers from the Royal Astronomical Society of Canada, who bring their telescopes to the mountaintop site most Saturday evenings
- walk through the Rockland neighbourhood of stately homes built around the turn of the 20th century, including a visit to Craigdarroch Castle,

built by self-made coal entrepreneur Robert Dunsmuir for his wife, Joan
- picnic, chat with military re-enactors and tour the restored buildings at Fort Rodd Hill and the adjacent Fisgard Lighthouse
- visit the Victoria Art Gallery, then walk a few blocks along Rockland Avenue to tour the gardens and grounds of Government House, the residence of BC's Lieutenant-Governor
- walk along the Gorge Waterway path network or rent a kayak to paddle the waterway up to Portage Inlet
- take a day or weekend cycle tour of the Saanich Peninsula on the Lochside Trail or tour the West Shore on the Galloping Goose Trail all the way to the old gold-mining camp of Leechtown
- plan a day to swim, hike, kayak, canoe or picnic at Thetis Lake Park, a wilderness oasis in View Royal
- watch a cricket game at the Beacon Hill Park pitch, a baseball game in Royal Athletic Park or a rugby game at Macdonald Park in James Bay or at the University of Victoria fields
- play a round of golf at one of the south island's famous courses, including Uplands Golf Club and the seaside Victoria Golf Club
- attend a powwow or war canoe races at the Tsartlip First Nation reserve on Brentwood Bay
- drive from Sidney to Jordan River, with many stops for short walks and delicious snacks; if you complete the circle route through Port Renfrew to Cowichan Lake and Duncan, drive south to Mill Bay and take the crossing on the small car ferry back to Brentwood Bay in Central Saanich

So what do long-time Victoria residents themselves do on a lazy weekend? As often as not, they look for activities that are both fun and free, though some venues accept donations. For example:

- concerts by visiting musicians on the Inner Harbour's lower causeway on summer evenings
- a lifetime's worth of scenic walking paths, hiking trails and cycle routes, which crisscross every part of the south island; some include challenging hill climbs, panoramic views, unspoiled seashore or other treasures

• concerts and recitals held at Christ Church Cathedral, the Victoria Conservatory of Music and in the University of Victoria music department

• beaches below the high-tide line are open to everyone, though some landowners attempt to block or hide access paths; never trespass on private property to get to the beach

• stargazing on summer Saturday evenings on Observatory Hill through telescopes provided by Royal Astronomical Society of Canada volunteers

• the Saturday evening fireworks displays at Butchart Gardens are visible from the west shore of the Saanich Peninsula, where residents quietly assemble on docks and moored boats in Brentwood Bay to watch the show

How do you spot a long-time Victorian? Look again at the young hiker in a Cowichan sweater worn almost transparent and proudly inherited from grandparents, wearing a "tin hat" of oiled canvas. Consider the old trouts in well-pressed woollens with only a discreet moth hole or two stepping out for a modest meal at the Bay's upstairs dining room or the Princess Mary. Listen to anyone who describes things as cultus (no-good) or skookum (powerful). Check out anyone sitting on a plaid car rug in Beacon Hill Park or on a local beach, sipping green tea from a battered "Stanley steamer" thermos. Note the people at Ross Bay Cemetery and Pioneer Square putting flowers on graves that don't bear famous names. Wait for the late for class driver backing his car around UVic's one-way Ring Road to catch a parking space. See the girl wearing a T-shirt from Smoking Lily, the city's smallest store, that depicts telephone poles or insects. And during the next big southeaster, note the otherwise sane and respectable folks who cycle through the wave curl at Ross Bay on Dallas Road, soaked to the skin and screaming in delight.

The Fairmont Empress is famous for its decadent high tea.

Here today, gone in an hour: the art of sidewalk chalk.

Author's Note

Victoria was unknown territory to me as a kid growing up in Saanich, since I rarely got past Cadboro Bay in one direction or Mount Douglas in the other. Bastion Square, Fan Tan Alley and the old provincial museum seemed mysterious and magical places even when I worked in the cannery near the Blue Bridge. When I returned to the south island after 24 years away, I found the city and its sister municipalities had lost none of their seductive charm.

The greatest delight of writing this book was the opportunity to rediscover Metchosin's orchards, the peninsula fields in morning mist, Oak Bay's gourmet shopping, the narrow streets of Esquimalt, all the nooks and crannies of a gold-rush city turned respectable. I met people from every continent who have put down new roots here; their love of the city and the island illuminated my research.

My thanks to every chance-met person who pointed out a feature, but especially to those who took me in hand and showed me the way: Bill Stavdal—whose knowledge encompasses Oak Bay and View Royal history, glaciation, geology and many other topics—Tove Barlow of Esquimalt, Oak Bay archivist Jean Sparks and researcher Annie Mayse. Stephen Hume kept me entertained with island lore and came to the rescue with last-minute fact checking. I owe a debt of gratitude to the writers of many fine books on Victoria and the south island, many of them listed in Resources, but above all to Danda Humphreys.

Warm thanks to editor Pam Robertson, who flagged every false note and graciously fine-tuned the ensemble, to Anna Comfort and the other dedicated staffers of Harbour Publishing, which has inspired an extraordinary generation of books in BC.

Photographer's Note

As a youngster growing up in other parts of Canada I loved escaping the urban scene for cottage country. When I transferred out to the University of Victoria in the late 70s it was a revelation: Salmon fishing at daybreak, before classes. Beach picnics below campus at Cadboro Bay or Willows Beach. Miles of country bike trails. Wildlife—eagles, whales, sea lions. Scuba diving, hiking and all sorts of new explorations—all at our doorsteps. So, after a childhood of living in six different cities and towns, I discovered Victoria and have made Sidney/North Saanich my home ever since.

Ultimately, my quest to share the splendour and delights of Victoria and the Island became expressed through photography. Although the scope of this expression has extended in many different directions since, I am grateful to this wonderful and vibrant area for my livelihood, family, community and home. Thanks to my family for understanding my restless wanderings with camera gear.

Some of my most delightful discoveries about BC were through Harbour Publishing's *Raincoast Chronicles*. So, I am delighted to work with the team at Harbour to contribute to this volume on Victoria. I hope the readers find some inspiration to discover the delights of Victoria and areas around.

Resources

Books

Adams, John. *Old Square-Toes and His Lady: The Life of James and Amelia Douglas.* Victoria: Horsdal & Schubart, 2001.

Barnes, Fred, ed. *Only in Oak Bay.* Oak Bay: Corporation of the District of Oak Bay, 1981.

Broadland, David, ed. *The Victoria Newcomers' Guide,* 3rd ed. Victoria: Campbell Communi-cations, 2001.

Castle, Geoffrey, ed. *Saanich: An Illustrated History.* Saanich: Corporation of the District of Saanich, 1989.

Clark, Brenda, Nicole Kilburn and Nick Russell, eds. *Victoria Underfoot.* Madeira Park, BC: Harbour Publishing, 2008.

Duffus, Maureen, ed. *Beyond the Blue Bridge.* Esquimalt: Esquimalt Silver Threads Writing Group, 1990.

Gibbs, James A. *Shipwrecks off Juan de Fuca.* Portland, OR: Binford & Mort, 1968.

Green, Valerie. *If These Walls Could Talk: Victoria's Houses from the Past.* Victoria: Touchwood Editions, 2001.

Green, Valerie, and Geoffrey Castle, eds. *Saanich Centennial, 1906–2006: 100 years, 100 stories.* Saanich: Corporation of the District of Saanich, 2005.

Humphreys, Danda. *Building Victoria.* Surrey, BC: Heritage House, 2004.

Humphreys, Danda. *On the Street Where You Live,* Vols. 1, 2 and 3. Surrey, BC: Heritage House, 2001.

Jenness, Diamond. "The Saanich Indians of Vancouver Island." Unpublished ms, Royal BC Museum n.d. [c. 1930s].

Johannesson, Kathy, transcrib., ed. and comp. *That Was Our Way of Life: Memories of Susan Lazzar Johnson, T'Sou-ke Elder.* Sooke: Sooke Region Museum, 1990.

Jupp, Ursula. *Cadboro: A Ship, A Bay, A Sea-Monster, 1842–1958.* Victoria: publ. by author, 1988.

Jupp, Ursula. *From Cordwood to Campus in Gordon Head: 1852 to 1959.* Victoria: publ. by author, 1975.

Jupp, Ursula. *Home Port Victoria.* Victoria: publ. by author, 1967.

Lansdowne, Helen. *Nature Walks Around Victoria.* Vancouver: Greystone Books, 1999.

Laurie, Sandra, Darlene George and Francine George, comps. *Legends of T'Sou-ke and West Coast Bands.* Sooke: Sooke Region Museum, 1978.

Mills, Donald C. *Giant Cedars, White Sands: Juan de Fuca Marine Trail Guidebook.* Sooke: Pallas-Trine Services, 1999.

Murdoch, G. "A History of the Municipality of Oak Bay." Oak Bay: unpublished ms, 1968.

Peers, Elida, ed. *A Guide to the Sooke Region.* Sooke: Sooke Region Museum, 2001.

Poth, Janet, ed. *Saltwater People: as told by Elliot, Dave Sr.,* 2nd ed. Saanich: Native Education, School District 63, 1990.

Pritchard, Allan, ed. *Vancouver Island Letters of Edmund Hope Verney: 1862–65.* Vancouver: UBC Press, 1996.

Reksten, Terry. *More English than the English: A very social history of Victoria.* Victoria: Orca Book Publishing, 2001.

Ringuette, Janis. "Beacon Hill Park History: 1842–2008." Available at www.beaconhillparkhistory.org.

Robinson, Sherri K. *Esquimalt Streets and Roads: A History.* Esquimalt: publ. by author, 1995.

Stranix, Dorothy. *Notes and Quotes: A Brief Historical Record of Colwood, Langford, Metchosin, Happy Valley-Glen Lake on Southern Vancouver Island.* N.p.: Joint Centennial Committee, n.d. [ca. 1960s].

Suttles, Wayne. *Coast Salish Essays.* Vancouver: Talon-books, 1987.

Teague, Jarrett Thomas. *Sacred Heart: John Dean Provincial Park.* Saanich: John Dean Nature House, 2004.

Turner, Robert D. *Vancouver Island Railroads,* 4th ed. San Marino, CA: Golden West Books, 1981.

Verney, Edmund Hope. *Vancouver Island Letters of Edmund Hope Verney, 1862–65.* Vancouver: UBC Press, 1996.

Virgin, Victor E. *History of North and South Saanich: Pioneers and District,* 2nd ed. Saanich: Saanich Pioneers Society, 1978.

Ward, Robin. *Echoes of Empire: Victoria & Its Remarkable Buildings.* Madeira Park, BC: Harbour Publishing, 1996.

Weston, Jim, and David Stirling, eds. *The Naturalist's Guide to the Victoria Region.* Victoria: Victoria Natural History Society, 1986.

Yorath, Chris. *The Geology of Southern Vancouver Island.* Madeira Park, BC: Harbour Publishing, 2005.

Maps

Sutherst, Jennifer. *Lost Streams of Victoria*. Victoria: South Island Aquatic Stewardship Society and Fisheries and Oceans Canada, 2003.

Websites

BC Association of Farmers' Markets: www.bcfarmersmarket.org

BC Geographical Names: http://archive.ilmb.gov.bc.ca/bcnames

BC Parks: www.env.gov.bc.ca/bcparks

BCStats: www.bcstats.gov.bc.ca

BC Tourism (HelloBC): www.hellobc.com

Beacon Hill Park—"A Walk on the Wild Side" by Agnes Lynn: http://friendsofbeaconhillpark.ca/walk_on_the_wild_side.htm

The Butchart Gardens: www.butchartgardens.com

Capital Regional District: www.crd.bc.ca

Congregation Emanu-El: www.congregation-emanu-el.org

Dictionary of Canadian Biography Online: www.biographi.ca

Dogwood Initiative: http://dogwoodinitiative.org

Environment Canada: www.ec.gc.ca

Farm Folk/City Folk: www.ffcf.bc.ca

First Voices: www.firstvoices.com

Fisgard Lighthouse Historical Site: www.fisgardlighthouse.com

Friends of Bowker Creek: http://members.shaw.ca/bowkercreek

Glendale Gardens & Woodland: www.glendalegardens.ca

Greater Victoria Sports Hall of Fame: www.gvshof.ca

Hatley Castle: www.hatleycastle.com

Heritage Oak Bay: www.heritageoakbay.ca

Herzberg Institute of Astrophysics: www.nrc-cnrc.gc.ca/eng/ibp/hia.html

History of Racialisation Group (HORG): "Imperial Paradise? An Alternative Walking Tour of Victoria, BC" by John Lutz et al. Available at: http://web.uvic.ca/walktour/index.html

Oak Bay Encyclopedia: www.webturf.com/oakbay/history/encyclopedia

Oak Bay Tea Party: www.oakbayteaparty.com

Oak Bay Tourism: "Walking Tours in Oak Bay." Available at www.oakbaytourism.com/activities/land/walking_tours.htm

Saanich Indian School Board: www.sisb.bc.ca

Songhees Nation: www.songheesnation.com

Southern Vancouver Island Growers: www.islandfarmfresh.com

Statistics Canada: www.statcan.gc.ca/start-debut-eng.html

Tourism Victoria: www.tourismvictoria.com

Travel with Taste: Indulgent Culinary Adventures: www.travelwithtaste.com

Tribal Journeys: http://tribaljourneys.wordpress.com

Vancouver Island Garden Trail: www.vancouverislandgardentrail.com

Index

Text Copyright © 2010 Susan Mayse
All photographs copyright Chris Cheadle, except where noted

1 2 3 4 5 — 14 13 12 11 10

Harbour Publishing Co. Ltd.
P.O. Box 219, Madeira Park, BC, V0N 2H0
www.harbourpublishing.com

Edited by Pam Robertson
Index by Erin Schopfer
Map by Roger Handling, Terra Firma Digital Arts
Text design by Roger Handling
Printed on FSC-certified paper containing a combination of fibres from well-managed forests and post-consumer recycled content
Printed and bound in China

Harbour Publishing acknowledges financial support from the Government of Canada through the Canada Book Fund and the Canada Council for the Arts, and from the Province of British Columbia through the BC Arts Council and the Book Publishing Tax Credit.

Library and Archives Canada Cataloguing in Publication

Mayse, Susan, 1948-
    Victoria : crown jewel of British Columbia : including Esquimalt, Oak Bay, Saanich and the Peninsula / Susan Mayse ; photos by Chris Cheadle.

Includes index.
ISBN 978-1-55017-503-5

    1. Victoria Region (B.C.)—Pictorial works. I. Cheadle, Chris, 1957-
II. Title.

FC3846.37.M39 2010   971.1'28050222   C2010-904248-4